MW01193876

PEOPLE AND THINGS
THAT WENT BEFORE

A Collection of Memories
(Fond and Otherwise)

Leonard Stegmann

People and Things That Went Before
Copyright © by Leonard Stegmann
All rights reserved
Including the right of reproduction
In whole or in part in any form.

CONTENTS

PREFACE

When I first began to read my mom got me a subscription to a magazine called *Children's Digest*. And while I can't say I read every issue cover to cover, I have no doubt that I read every single joke and riddle. And it's my particular gift/curse that I remember them all. Even today when some little smartass asks me a riddle that he thinks was just created that day, I always shock him by knowing the answer. For example, do you know what a blue hat becomes when you throw it into the Red Sea? Wet!

My attraction to joke books was an early sign that I would become a writer of humor. But humor is a funny thing. (I just made that up.) In collecting the essays for this collection I find most of them fall into one of three categories. First, there are the stories that were funny when they happened and continued to be over the years, such as the one about my hapless little brother that begins this book. Then there are those that are funny now but certainly weren't when they occurred. I still can't believe what that girl said when I called her on New Year's Eve! And finally, those that are not funny, never were and never will be. These stories are sad, inevitable and a part of life. All of our lives.

We often hear that we shouldn't live in the past. "Live in the moment!" is today's ubiquitous mantra. And I think that's good advice. Still, which of us can resist the look back, the quick over-the-shoulder glance down the road we have travelled; taking our eyes off, for just a second, where we're going to remember and marvel at where we've been. No, it's probably not very healthy to live in the past, but surely there can be no harm in the occasional visit.

Leonard Stegmann
Half Moon Bay, California

My Brother's Favorite Story

This was one of my brother's favorite stories from when we were kids. He often requested to hear it and seemed to thoroughly enjoy it every time I told it; which I think says a lot about his character, since in the story he turns out to be the butt of the joke.

When I was about six and my brother about four our grandfather took us to a local park. Now, as any kid knows, when you go for a ride in a car the most important thing in the world is making sure that you get a window seat. And so, being the big brother that I was, when my grandfather unlocked and opened the passenger door I looked at my brother and ordered, "You get in first."

He obediently climbed in and slid over to sit next to Grandpa. I then climbed in and, secure in my choice position by the window, proceeded to enjoy the changing view as we made our way to the park, oblivious, of course, to my brother's suffering as he endured the dreaded middle seat.

I don't remember what we did at the park that day. I assume we played on the swings and the slide and ran amok and made a lot of noise. I *do* vaguely remember watching some "big kids" as they sat around a picnic table playing "knock-hockey," an ancient and primitive board game that you could not possibly have ever played. Or even heard of.

After a few hours of wild abandon it was time to leave, and as Grandpa unlocked and opened the car door you could feel the wheels in my brother's four-year-old head begin to turn. "OK, Lenny, this time *you* get in the car first!" he said with all the firm resolve that a younger brother is capable of mustering.

Fair's fair, and with a smile I gleefully hopped into the car and slid across the seat. My brother, feeling quite triumphant I'm sure, followed close behind while I waited in delicious anticipation for realization to dawn. You should have seen the look of absolute confusion on my little brother's face when my grandfather got into the car and my brother found himself once again stuck in the middle. You see, this time my grandfather had opened the door on the *driver's* side.

My First Beatles Record: A Confession

I had to be talked into buying my first Beatles record. Let me repeat that: I, Leonard Stegmann, without a doubt the biggest and most resolute Beatles fan in the entire world, and probably the universe, had to be talked into buying my first Beatles record. That's an absolutely astounding confession, isn't it?

The person who convinced me to buy the record was my mother. In truth it was more than convincing; her method approached strong-arm tactics. You see, my brother and I had each gotten a dollar for Easter, and we were now shopping with Mom and trying to decide what to get with our unexpected windfall. Scoff if you will, but back then, and with me only eleven years old, a dollar was nothing to be taken lightly. My financial holdings so far had consisted mostly of loose change--nickels, dimes and the occasional quarter--but a dollar catapulted me into a whole new fiscal stratum entirely. This was *folding* money.

My brother was already holding his record, a 45 of the Beatles' *I Want to Hold Your Hand.* I was still hemming and hawing, clutching my now-sweaty dollar to my chest, when my Mom gave me something of a verbal shove, suggesting that I get the other one. The "other one" was *She Loves You*, which was and remains one of the Beatles' biggest hits.I often wondered why my mom pushed for my brother and me to buy those records. It was, remember, at the height of Beatlemania and I've long suspected that it was her way of being a part of the excitement. At thirty-six she was, of course, much too ancient to participate directly in the hysteria, but at maybe by encouraging her sons to buy a couple of Beatles records she at least could stand on the fringes and peer in.

And yet this theory is in direct contrast with what my mother told me not so very long ago. She explained how, at the time, parents were actually afraid of the Beatles, terrified that, with their alien hair and even more alien music, they were some freakish Pied Pipers come to steal their children.

I would, of course, go on to acquire every Beatles album that was produced, only to buy them all again years later when they were released on compact disc. And to think it all started with one eighty-eight cent semi-forced purchase in a record store nearly half a century ago. Incidentally, I still have that copy of *She Loves You* (on the Swan label!) although I don't have the sleeve. For some reason that I can't begin to imagine, at some point I gathered all the jackets to my Beatles 45's, colorful photos and all, and threw them out. I think I believed this somehow "streamlined" my collection.

And now, at this stage of my life, my most fervent hope is that I live long enough to see the invention of a workable time machine. I'd very much like to go back to that long-ago era, find that young Beatles fan who threw away all the record covers, and give him a swift and well-deserved kick in the ass.

Jimmy Did It

Looking back through the fog of fifty years, I still can't believe that I did such a thing. Back then such an act was completely out of character, just as it would be today. I've really never been capable of such a ballsy move at any point in my life, much less at the age of seven. Then again, the truth is I didn't really do it. Jimmy did.

I've recently noticed a peculiar gap in my mental abilities. (Only recently? you ask in that cute way of yours that makes me want to slap the back of your head.) For the longest time I've been able to name every one of my grammar school teachers, right from the beginning. For example, in kindergarten I was taught by Miss Weisseglass and Miss Glasner. "We have two glasses in the class!" I had quipped aloud back then. Give me a break--I was five.

I remember Mrs. C from first grade and of course Mrs. Q from second grade. (I love the way I use just their initials, as if I'm afraid that my old educators are going to rise up out of their graves and sue me.) The reason Mrs. Q. earns the "of course" is that she's the bit-, I mean teacher, who announced to me, and to all my second grade classmates, that there was no such thing as Santa Claus. Not that I'm still holding a grudge. Ahem.

But Mrs. Q was only my second grade teacher for the first half of the school year. It was then that my family moved from Queens to the wilds of Long Island, and were nice enough to bring me along. And here's where I draw the blank. Who was my teacher for the second half of the year, once I had started school on Long Island?

It's not a complete blank, but it's not a solid memory either. I have a name in mind and an oh-so-vague image of a skinny woman in a drab dress and 60's style horn-rimmed glasses. Was she my teacher? I'm just not sure, but for the sake of this tale let's say she was. And let's call her Mrs. T.

And here again I must apologize for gaps in my memory, and thus in the story. I don't remember what we did exactly, but one day Mrs. T sent both Jimmy and I to the principal's office. Now there's still a part of me that feels this couldn't have possibly happened. I was a good student and a well-behaved follower of the rules to boot. And Jimmy, who I would become rather close friends with for a while in high school, was nothing short of brilliant. And yet here we were, banished from our classroom and trudging down the long, empty hallway to meet our fate. What could we have possibly done?

Sadly, I'll never know and neither will you. What I do know is that the heavy hand of doom was gripping me hard as we got closer and closer to the principal's office. We were almost at the door, and I was having hellish visions of my parents being called to the school to be told of my insidious crime, when Jimmy shook his head and signaled for me to follow him. Then we walked down another hallway and basically took a stroll around the school.

"What manner of self-destructive insanity is this?" I thought to myself. In little kid's words, of course. What is Jimmy doing? Is he trying to get us expelled? Is he trying to get us sent to prison? And why, oh why, am I following him. I hardly know him. Hell, I'm new here--I hardly know anybody!

But alas, there was no turning back now. I did what Jimmy told me to do and when he had deemed enough time had passed we simply headed back to our classroom. We slowly opened the door and I suddenly knew what it must have felt like to be a first-wave soldier landing on Omaha Beach on D-Day. OK, no I didn't, not even close. But I was still terrified as I contemplated what fate awaited me behind that pale-green door. (And no, I wasn't worried about Jimmy. Fuck him. He's the lunatic who had gotten me into this mess in the first place.)

Mrs. T. looked up from the book she was reading aloud and with the tiniest of gestures indicated that we should take our seats. And, wearing long-faced looks of contrition that announced to the world that we had indeed been thoroughly and mercilessly reprimanded by the principal, we did just that.

And that was the end of it. Nothing ever happened. Oh sure, to this day I'll cringe a bit every time the phone rings, knowing in my heart that my act of deceit has finally been uncovered and it's time to pay for my crime. And yet I'll never completely understand how we got away with it.

Didn't Mrs. T. and the principal ever speak to each other? Didn't the topic ever come up, even for a laugh, between cigarette-induced coughing fits in the teacher's lounge? Why didn't Mrs. T. at least pick up the classroom phone and call to see how it went, and if my cohort and I had truly suffered enough? I'll never know. And so I'll forever file this episode under the heading, "The time I actually got away with something." And believe me, it was the only time.

Panty Raid at the Dawn of Feminism

I'm reading a book about what goes on behind the scenes at sororities. I know, I know. It was in a stack of free books someone had left out across the street and so it became mine. It was the only one I took. I originally just intended to "peruse" it before starting to read the next novel on my pile, but hey, it's got young women, booze, drugs, sex…what's not to like?

Although the book is a report on the mysterious goings-on at sororities from just a few years ago, sororities and fraternities always seemed to me to be hopeless anachronisms, like something right out of the Ricky and David Nelson malt shop era. And as such reading about them reminded me of another anachronism of college life: the panty raid.

Even back in 1971, when I first heard the rumors about panty raids circulating though the dorm, I thought that the concept was something of a throwback to the fifties. It amazes me now to think that when I was a freshman in college the fifties had only come to an end eleven years earlier. It had seemed so long ago at the time.

And if I may be perfectly honest, I'm not sure I even knew what a panty raid was back then. If I may be even more honest, I'm not sure that I know now. I'm resisting the temptation to look up the actual definition on the web.

Lord knows I love the Internet, but sometimes I wonder if it is perhaps taking the mystery out of everything.

The rumor was that our dorm, Kent Hall, was going to stage a panty raid on the women's dorm next door, name forgotten. When I began to understand that a panty raid was not something akin to a sexual orgy but rather a bunch of guys running around like wildmen stealing women's underwear I was pretty sure it was not something of which I wanted to be a part. I didn't get it and frankly it sounded aggressive and barbaric. And illegal. It's stealing, isn't it? Even at that impressionable age I knew that I didn't want to steal panties from young women; I wanted to *remove* panties from young women.

Later that evening a gang (for that is what they were) of my dorm-mates returned from the "hunt" and decorated our hallway with a lacy assortment of the purloined bras and panties. There was much whooping and hollering, a celebration probably not unlike a successful tribe returning to the fire with a slain wooly mammoth.

Eventually things calmed down, as they always will, and when it seemed as if everything was about back to normal another rumor began to spread: The women in the dorm next door, name of dorm forgotten, were planning a retaliation. They were coming by that night in a revenge attack that was being referred to as a "jock raid."

Oh my goodness gracious! Should I get up and lock the door? After all, I hadn't done anything wrong, but so what? The pages of history are written in the blood of innocent victims, yes? And so now years later I see no shame in admitting that on that night years ago yes, I was scared and yes, I did get up to lock the door.

I needn't have worried. The threatened jock raid never occurred. My jock as well as the rest of my dainty underthings remained safely in my dresser drawer. And they remained mine. As it turned out only one woman ventured into our dorm that night. She had long straight hippie-hair that was secured with a headband, wore granny glasses, sandals and, ironically, no bra. She carried a large cardboard box and calmly walked down the hallway, stopping occasionally to remove a pair of panties from a light fixture or a brassiere that was hanging unceremoniously from an Exit sign.

"These things are very expensive," she explained calmly and to no one in particular. And, after all the garments had been cleared from the hallway, she left.

The Hat

And tonight I present yet another way we can divide people into two categories. For this one let's set the way-back machine to eighth grade, and more specifically to one of the many after school eighth grade dances I attended.

And that's exactly what I did—attended. My memory is a bit foggy but I'm pretty sure that I went to at least a dozen of these hormone-driven rituals and yet never danced a single dance. Hey, I said I could divide the world into two main groups; I didn't say that I was cool.

So there I am in my usual place high atop the bleachers, watching most of the girls and several of the boys dance to electrified music of a band made up of four of my classmates. (All of the bands had four back then. Why? Because the Beatles had four, silly.) And so I sat atop my perch, too shy to dance, and listened to the music of four guys my own age who not only were not too shy to dance but had no trouble standing up in front of the entire school singing and playing instruments.

I don't remember the name of the lead singer of the band. I recall that he didn't play a guitar but only sang, and that I was surprised to see him up on the stage because up until that afternoon I had known him only as one of the school thugs. He was a low-brow and a bully, and I think he even smoked. But there he was giving it his all up on the stage, singing his foul black heart out into the microphone. I gave him credit.

I also recall that he was wearing a hat as he performed. Some of you may know that John Lennon sometimes wore a Greek fisherman-type hat while the other Beatles did not. It was an early show of individualism from one of four young men who up until then had been viewed as a single living organism: the Beatles.

The singing thug had obviously been influenced by Lennon, and clearly understood the axiom which states that one member of a band wearing a cap is infinitely cooler than all four wearing a cap. One person who definitely did *not* see it that way was the school's gruff and unyielding assistant principal.

I watched from my outpost in the bleachers as the white-haired old fart spoke to the thug. I later learned that he had asked if the hat was part of the band's "uniform." When told it was not he commanded the thug take it off, which he did, and the dance continued.

In his mind I'm sure the assistant principal felt that he was being quite fair, even liberal. If every member of the band had been wearing a hat, well sure, it was obviously part of their costume and perfectly acceptable, like a Catholic school uniform. But only one guy wearing a hat smacked of subversion and rebellion, and *that* needed to be quashed immediately. And so it was.

So we can see that people can be divided into two groups: the ones who rise, proclaim, create and wear hats while singing in a band and those who suppress, oppress, destroy and force people to take off that damn hat, and I mean *now,* mister! How about you—do *you* understand why one member of a band wearing a hat is cool? If not I think we've established to which group you belong. In fact there might be an exciting future waiting for you in the lucrative assistant principal business.

Tales of Unspeakable Woe: The Dalmatian

I never knew where he came from. I only know that one day a Dalmatian---a fire dog we used to call them-- appeared in our backyard. He was full-grown and friendly and we hit it off immediately. I was only four years old at the time, and so the dog, even on all fours, was taller than my waist. On his hind legs he would have dwarfed me.

Oh, but we had fun that day! We were inseparable, and went everywhere together. Which of course wasn't very far considering my tender age and associated travel restrictions. Still, finding entertaining ways to pass the time in the front yard and then in the backyard was more than enough to fill a young boy's day. Especially if he now had a wonderful new dog to play with.Sometime in the afternoon Mom asked me to go next door to pick up something from our neighbor, Mrs. Massa. What is was I can no longer remember, nor should I be expected to after over half a century. Flour? Sugar? It's not important. What *is* important is that my new-found spotted friend went with me.

Together we walked around the back of Mrs. Massa's house and up her red-painted brick "stoop." I knocked politely on her door, which is something children did back then, and she handed me whatever that item might have been. I said good-bye, politely, and turned to descend the brick staircase, as did the Dalmatian. Almost immediately our legs got tangled--there were six of them, after all--and I tumbled down the stairs. I lay there stunned for a few seconds until I realized I was unhurt, picked myself up and proceeded to run home, crying all the way.

Sometime later I was sitting inside on a step in the entryway by our side door, still mad at the world and especially at my former canine friend, who I believed had betrayed me. I was also still crying and sniffling, feeling about as sorry for myself as a human being of any age is capable, when the Dalmatian came up to the screen door. I remember his searching eyes and snuffling nose on the other side of the screen, as he used his keen senses to track down his lost friend. He didn't know what had happened or where I had gone; all he knew for sure was it was a bright and sunny day and he was ready to play some more.

But I, I was having none of it. The dog who I had thought was my friend had caused me to fall, and that to me was unforgivable. I stood up and approached the door, the Dalmatian's tail wagging in anticipation of my approach. I slammed the outer door in his face, yelling at him with all the energy a four-year-old can muster.

"Go away!" I screamed.

A short time later I was feeling somewhat soothed, having mostly recovered from my terrible ordeal. I went outside and looked in the backyard. Then I walked around the side of the house and looked in the front yard. The Dalmatian was nowhere to be found, and I knew that I had no-one to blame but myself. I had told him, loudly and clearly, to go away and he had. And he never came back again.

The Give-A-Show Projector

I was recently reminded of a day many years ago when I was ten and my brother was either about or exactly eight. By exactly I mean to the day, because it was either his birthday or a day or two before it. And I had a plan.

My brother wanted a Give-A-Show Projector for his birthday. If you don't remember, or never knew, what a Give-A-Show Projector was just hop on over to Ebay, where you'll find no less than six of them up for auction. Remarkably you can get one, still in the box, for under fifty bucks. Yes, that's complete with the slides.

For those of you too lazy to look, the Give-A-Show Projector was basically a glorified flashlight through which you could feed a strip of seven celluloid cartoon panels and project them onto the wall, telling a story. The strips included such classic characters as Popeye, Yogi Bear, Rocky and Bullwinkle, Huckleberry Hound, Lassie, Auggie Doogie—all the greats. And if I appear to be making light of it I must apologize—the Give-A-Show Projector was a pretty cool thing to own. In fact I came closer than I care to admit to bidding on one today.

Ah yes, the plan. I knew my brother had asked for the projector for his birthday. On this Saturday my parents had gone out shopping and the gears in my head were turning. Let's put on a show in the garage! The timing was a little tricky, but I figured by the time I had sold the nickel tickets to the neighborhood kids and got them seated in the garage my parents would be back with the projector and the show could begin.

By now you might be wondering why I was the one who got to run the show and make money when the projector was a gift for my brother. The answer to that is twofold: First, the show was *my* brainchild. I made it up, sold the tickets and planned every stage of the operation. Why, one might call me the P.T. Barnum of Windhorst Avenue! And second, I was the older brother, so enough said about that.

How many tickets did we sell that day? I would guess that there were no less than ten paying customers perched on rickety old chairs in that fumey garage, waiting for the show to begin. My sales technique had worked like a charm, but now I was starting to sweat. It was clearly now show time and there was no sign of my parents. Where the hell were they? How could they do this to me, uh, I mean my brother?

Finally, just before things were about to turn ugly, I saw the white Bel-Air turn the corner. Saved! I rushed out to greet my parents as they got out of the car, possibly the first time I ever did. "Do you have the Give-A-Show Projector?" I asked, desperately trying to remain cool in the face of my building anxiety. My parents, as you've already anticipated, looked at me as if I had asked them if they'd remembered the pterodactyl eggs. And then they went in the house.

I don't recall, but I assume I refunded all the money. Maybe I didn't. Maybe I substituted some bullshit live show and saved the day. I wouldn't put it past me. But apparently I learned a valuable lesson that day, a lesson I could have learned much less painfully simply by remembering the old saying, "Don't count your chickens," etc. etc.

Tatelah

When I noticed that the number of this posting is the same as the number of kids in my high school graduation class, well, of course it connected. Numbers, useless facts, bits of memories—they never seem to disappear, at least not from *my* brain. And that, Kiddies, is how you get an eleven year headache.

The valedictorian of my high school class was a friend of mine. We were never close friends, but we were both part of loose association of acquaintances who had come up from grade school through high school together. He was a nice guy.

Way back then, 1971 to pinpoint the year for you, it was the style for the valedictorian of each school to give a speech that was somewhat controversial in nature. Hey, the Vietnam War was raging, many kids our age or a little older were dying, and something had to be said.

Our valedictorian, like most of my high school friends, was a pudgy and pleasant middle-class Jewish kid. He was no anti-war radical, but he certainly wasn't a supporter. Almost nobody was by 1971. It was finally being recognized as a dead-end war that had wasted untold numbers of innocent lives. Luckily those days are long gone, eh?

Some of the kids in my group had a nickname for our valedictorian friend. It was a Jewish word: tatelah. Well, that's not a Jewish word—I don't think there is such a thing. It's either Yiddish or Hebrew and, even after all these years and all those Jewish friends, I'm a little embarrassed to admit that I still don't know the difference.

Which would surprise the many well-meaning and not-so-well-meaning people who have confronted me over the course of my life and questioned me as to whether I was Jewish. Others have even gone so far as to *insist* I was Jewish. No, it wasn't like 1939 Germany, but it wasn't impossible to connect the dots, either. But I'm not Jewish, and we've already covered this topic in a previous article. I believe it boasted the clever title *I'm Not Jewish.*

And because I'm not Jewish I've never completely understood the reason for calling our friend tatelah. I know that the term is some form of diminutive endearment, like, "Are you hungry, tatelah?" but I never got an exact translation. Not even tonight when I searched all over the internet for its meaning. I even tried both an English-Yiddish dictionary and an English-Hebrew dictionary. No luck.

It may be hard to comprehend now, but there was a lot of pressure on our friend when he climbed up to the podium to give his valedictory address. Plus he had a fairly high voice, which would make his job twice as difficult. After all, even condemning Nixon as a war criminal loses some of its punch when delivered in a voice that sounds like it came out of Mickey Mouse.

Well, our friend didn't condemn Nixon as a war criminal. In fact I don't remember exactly what he said, but when the speech was over we all nodded our approval.

He had said the things that needed to be said, and he had done it in a strong, calm and intelligent manner. And I don't know how it is now, but back then it was not a common occurrence for cocky hormone-driven teen-aged punks like us to give a genuine compliment to one of our own. But we did. And why not? Our little tatelah had done real good.

Remembrance of Co-Workers Past

E-mail. It can be the 21st century equivalent of the telegram and it sometimes brings bad news. As it did that today: one of us has died.

It was Peachpit who recently pointed out what a unique situation it is. We are a group of former co-workers who still remain in touch with each other long after we've stopped working together. These are creative, talented people. Funny people. Once when I first began the job I did a Katherine Hepburn impression and immediately five people joined in with their own Katherine Hepburn impressions. Better ones. Our job was to make television commercials. I liked to call them "little movies."

It would be a cliché, and inaccurate, to call us a family. We're not a family. We're simply a group of people who once worked together for a period of time many years ago and have, by choice, remained in touch. We all seem to have the vague, almost indefinable feeling that we were once part of something special. We have a shared experience as a group, an experience we know we may never have again. We did good work and we had fun doing it.

I don't want to give the impression that our work environment was like the *Mary Tyler Moore Show*. It was a job and came with the requisite job bullshit. Each day we were forced to deal with irritating clients, soulless salespeople and outlandish deadlines. And each other.

There were always petty squabbles among us, conflicts that have diminished in importance with each passing year. But conflicts are to be expected in *any* job, because a job, as a rule, is not unlike a twisted experiment conducted by some deranged scientist, putting a couple of dozen people together in a artificially-lit building for eight hours a day. It's rats in a cage, except with 401k plans.

A few years ago there was a Monkees reunion show on TV. I believe it was Mickey Dolenz who was answering the critics who said that the Monkees were nothing more than a handpicked group of lightweights and were never a *real* rock group. Dolenz pointed out that, while the charges may be true, it was now thirty years later and they were doing a reunion show and still selling records. Therefore, no matter what you thought of the band, *something* must have happened.

I have a memory of years ago sitting in a circle in a backroom at work with eight or nine of my former co-workers. It was a slow day and soon the questions began to flow. They were thought-provoking questions at first, such as who would you invite to a dinner party if you could choose anyone in history. Jesus was big. So were the Beatles.

Then the questions got more personal. And sexier. At what age did you lose your virginity? What was the biggest age gap you've had with a lover? (I won that one, clocking in with an astounding 29 years. Don't ask.) The group discussion went on for over two hours and was a remarkably bonding, sharing experience--the kind managers dream of--and yet I can't imagine any other group of co-workers doing this without at least one person running to human resources crying sexual harassment.

There were days when we all went to have lunch at a local Chinese restaurant, cracking jokes and laughing like some low-rent Algonquin Round Table. And then there was the day when we huddled breathless around a small television set and emitted a collective gasp as the O.J. verdict was read. There were football bets and *Survivor* pools, and most days I went home with my face hurting from laughing all day.

Today I only see two or three of these people on a regular basis, but we all remain in touch via group e-mails. I find this remarkable, considering it's been nearly twenty years since I first began to meet, and five years since I've worked with, these people who would eventually, inevitably, become my former co-workers.

Sometimes I think that maybe we were just co-workers, thrown together against our wills by the common need to earn a living. But I don't think so, because here we are many years later, coming together once again to express our common sorrow because one of us has died. I can't pinpoint exactly why this collection of creative misfits has remained in touch as a group long after we have ceased to see each other on a daily basis. Perhaps it's the slow-dawning realization of having once belonged to something uniquely wonderful. Or maybe it's just like the Monkee said. *Something* happened.

Pictures of Yesterday

This feels strange. This feels *very* strange. A few days ago I was moving some pillows to grab my camera when I came across another camera, one that I did not recognize. It was small, silver but clearly not digital.

"Where did this camera come from?" I asked Spike.

"That was your brother's," she answered.

Oh.

It didn't seem possible that my brother's camera had lain in the corner of the bedroom, unseen and unknown, throughout the four years since he passed away. I opened it up and was almost more amazed to find that the battery was still working. There in the shot indicator was a digital number three. The camera had three pictures in it.

Or so I thought at first. Then I thought a little more about it and realized that the three most likely meant that it was ready to take the third shot, indicating that there were, at the most, two pictures on the film. Two pictures taken by my brother over four years ago—most likely the last ones he ever took. I had to get them developed.

I rewound the film and brought it to Longs. Feeling like the last person on Earth who still uses film, I dropped the roll into the envelope and the envelope into the slot. I even wrote a note that explained that there most likely would be two or less pictures on the roll.

I picked up the pictures today and right now am looking at the sealed envelope. I still have no clue what's in it, but I was somewhat surprised by the thickness of the envelope and the price of the developing, which came to $7.19. That seems like quite a bit to develop two pictures, but before I start ranting about overpricing I should find exactly what I have.

Tonight, like my Brussels sprouts and absinthe experiments, I'm going to share the results with you as they happen. Unlike those exercises, however, this one isn't fun. It's as if I'm receiving a message through time, a photographic missive from not that long ago but not that recent either. I'm aware that I'm hesitating now because, while I'm not sure what I'll see when I open the envelope, I can almost guarantee that it will make me sad. And nobody wants to be sad.

And now I'm going to open the envelope.

There *are* three pictures. They were obviously taken on some sort of camping trip. There is a fire and a tent. The first picture is of a long-haired, balding man who is sitting in a camping chair and holding a small dog in his arms, on its back like a baby. The other two pictures show various people sitting in camping chairs and smiling at the camera. I have no idea who these people are but they seem relaxed and happy. They are having a good time.

It's obviously my brother who is taking the pictures. He does not appear in any of the photos, and I am surprised to find that I am somewhat relieved by this. And I am somewhat disappointed as well.

My First Gig

The way I looked at it was simple: He was cheating and I was not. "He" was a dorm-mate name Jack who lived about two rooms down from me during my freshman year in college. Jack was not the best student and somehow we had come to an arrangement where I would write his English papers for him. The payment schedule we agreed on said that I would get $3 for every C, $4 for every B and $5 for every A.

Now what Jack was doing, paying someone else to write his papers, was to my way of thinking beyond despicable. He was clearly cheating. While I, doing extra work in addition to my own school assignments, was involved in something quite admirable. I was, after all, being paid for my writing—what could be nobler than that?

I don't remember many of the details. If I wrote more than five papers for Jack I'd be surprised. And I know I never got a grade lower than a B. The one detail I *do* recall was a comment that a teacher had written on one of the papers I had written for Jack. I can't recall it word for word, but the gist of it was that, although Jack's writing had recently improved quite a bit, it was still not enough to earn him a passing grade for the class.

I had two reactions after reading that short comment. First, I was bursting with pride that the teacher, Jack's teacher, would recognize how much better the writing was since I had taken over the assignments. My second reaction was a twisted sort of satisfaction. Jack would be failing his class, and well he should. He was, after all, a cheater.

There is a service I subscribe to that sends me writing assignments on a regular basis. Most are from businesses looking for advertising and website writing, but occasionally I'll see a description and immediately identify it as some college kid with more money than brains looking to have a paper written. I always turn them down. It's strange, but I guess nearly forty years after my first paid writing gig I now have some moral reservations about writing papers to help kids cheat. Besides, in many cases the offered pay is, sadly, on par with what I received from Jack in 1971.

Jack wasn't a close friend and I never saw him after we graduated. I did, however, hear about him years later. Apparently he had gone on to become a lawyer.

"I'm Hopeless"

Listen, as long as I still have the way-back machine plugged in I'm going to use it again tonight. This is another sports-related story that dates back to the misty recesses of my long-ago youth, but this one doesn't star me. It features my childhood pal Arthur.

I've written about Arthur previously on these pages but I don't think I've related this particular story. If I have and I'm repeating myself I apologize. Besides, I've written 350 of these damn things so if I cover the same ground once in a while cut me a little slack, OK?

Arthur, you may recall, was a close friend of mine from fifth grade right up until high school graduation. You may also recall that he is the only person on Earth that I've ever admitted might, *might*, be smarter than me.

Yes, in the classroom Arthur was indeed a wizard. If I remember correctly he went through high school taking nothing but Honors classes. (Unlike yours truly.) He also had a wicked sense of humor that perfectly complemented my own, which I suppose explains the friendship as much as anything else. Arthur did however have one flaw: he was a complete spaz.

In sixth grade our school held a sort of Recess Olympics. I certainly can't remember all the events (or what I had for breakfast this morning, for that matter) but I know there was a high jump, a hop, skip and jump and some inane relay race with wooden pins. Each student was required to compete in an event. Memories are suddenly rushing back. I believe that I personally competed in the relay race, which is surprising since it was the type of event usually reserved for only the swift. (Although today, ironically, my wife often tells me that I am indeed fast, although sadly not in a way that would win a schoolyard competition.)

There was also an event called the standing broad jump. It was the most basic of the tasks and was exactly what its name implied: The contestant started from a standing position and simply had to jump. It was a distance competition, the goal being, obviously, to see who could jump the farthest. As it seemed to require the least amount of athletic acumen, and perhaps even no coordination at all, this was the event that Arthur chose. Or had chosen for him.

I still remember where I was standing and at what angle when it came time for Arthur to make his jump. I watched my friend as he got into a slight squat, made his jump, tripped over his feet and fell to the ground. Within two seconds of hitting the pavement Arthur was up on his feet, embarrassed and with arms flailing, proclaiming loudly and disgustedly to the world, "I'm hopeless!"

Five years later Arthur, myself and two others from our group found ourselves sitting in the bleachers of the high school gym. This was the first meeting of those sophomores who had decided to try out for the school football team. The coach, who I had previously only known as my math teacher, was giving his recruitment speech about how great playing football was. He was making the point that when you hit a player from the other team and he went down it was "a better feeling than getting laid."

I tell you honestly at the age of 15 I had only the vaguest notion of exactly what "getting laid" was, but I was pretty sure it would feel a lot better than knocking down some dopey high school kid. (A few years later I was more qualified to research the coach's theory and so was able to confirm what I had only previously suspected—that guy was nuts.)

That meeting was the end of my high school football career. Of the other three of my group, one attended one practice and promptly joined me on the sidelines. The other two continued to attend practice, made the team and played the entire season. One of the two was Arthur.

I never did see Arthur play in a game. Nor did I see him after our freshman year in college. I've made attempts and have been unable to track him down, but I hope he's out there somewhere enjoying himself. I'm sure he's still smart and has accomplished a great deal with his life, but I suspect the season he played on the high school football team remains one of his proudest achievements. I never told him, but I too always thought it was pretty cool.

I Hated The Bourbon Barrel

Despite appearances to the contrary, I often do a little research before I begin one of these insightful missives. Tonight I took the trouble to search the Internet to see if The Bourbon Barrel could somehow still be in existence. I'm happy to report that apparently it isn't.

You would have loved the Bourbon Barrel. It was a homey kind of bar that my friends and I would go to during that short period of time between getting our driver's licenses and splitting for college. Yes, *you* would have loved it. I hated it.

Well, hate is an ugly word. But instead of softening my rhetoric let me describe the place to you. The Bourbon Barrel was indeed a local bar, although in what Long Island city it was located I've long forgotten and ceased to care. What made the Bourbon Barrel unique was that on weekends it provided "entertainment," and I'm laying heavy on those quotation marks.

If I remember correctly, and there is no reason to assume that I do, there were usually two or three performers on the makeshift stage, possibly a guitarist and a banjo player. Oh, and did I mention that all the songs were sing-alongs? And they were real old-timey cornball crap like "Daisy, Daisy" and "Has Anybody Seen My Gal?" Listen I'm not one to disparage the music of any generation but who at the age of eighteen, in the middle of Rock's greatest era when the Who and

Janis and the Doors strode the Earth, wanted to listen to that swill? Not me.

And if you're a regular reader you must have realized by now that I'm not big on sing-alongs or any other humiliating public displays that somehow pass for fun among others. I'm more the "sit alone in a dark room late at night and write bitter essays" type, in case you hadn't noticed. You want me to sit in a beer hall filled with drunken people singing, "I'm Looking Over A Four Leaf Clover"? I'd rather be water-boarded.

Oh, and speaking of which, and I ask you to remember I was an eighteen year old rebel during the Nixon administration at this time, there was a real patriotic mood at the Bourbon Barrel. At one point during the night the performers would bring out the flag that had been leaning against the wall and, as they unfurled it, begin to sing, "God Bless America." Soon the entire audience was standing on wobbly drunken legs and joining in, while my stomach knotted into a tight little monkey fist of anger. So apparently my staunch anti-patriotism stand pre-dates both of the Bush fiascos and could in fact possibly be a genetic mutation; and a positive one at that.

And once again remembering the times, the Bourbon Barrel was also a place where my parents and their friends liked to frequent. Now it was almost inconceivable to a teenager of that era that the two parties on either side of the generation gap could possibly enjoy the same entertainment. Why, that would be as if my dad had come into room smoking a joint and asked to borrow my *Led*

Zeppelin IV album. There were certain lines back then that could not and should not be crossed.

And yet I must confess that I went to the Bourbon Barrel on more than several occasions. I hated the songs, I hated the patriotism and I hated the alcohol-fueled wholesomeness. So why go? There were two reasons: First, for some reason that I'll have to ask him one of these days, my best friend liked it. He even sang along with the tunes. And two, well chicks, what did you think? There were chicks there--young, drunken chicks.

In closing, since I pride myself in being at least as fair and balanced as Fox News, I'm obligated to mention that there *was* one thing that I enjoyed about the Bourbon Barrel, and that was the big barrel itself. You see, it was filled with peanuts. Free peanuts. Peanuts you could eat all night long, and then drop the discarded shells right on the floor! That was wild stuff for a kid who grew up in a spic 'n' span and sparkly Long Island suburb where the lawns were edged, the leaves were raked and the snow was shoveled. Yeah, I really liked those peanuts.

Tales of Unspeakable Woe: The Found Wallet

It was one of those times when you look and then you look again. You're not really sure what you're seeing. But there it was, half open on a little pile of dirt near a patch of neglected plants in a forgotten corner of a gas station: an actual wallet.

I don't remember exactly why I was at a gas station to begin with, but at eight years old there could be but two conceivable reasons. I was there either to get air for my bicycle tire, which was free, or to buy a bottle of Orange Crush from a vending machine, which was a dime. You see, back then gas stations weren't the one-stop answer to all your needs that they were to become. You couldn't stop for gas and also pick up, say, a package of Swiss cheese or a bottle of Nyquil. I mean, the gas station I go to today actually sells *sushi*, for fuck's sake.

At first I thought the wallet must have been purposely discarded, seemingly tossed into that barren corner as it was. Once I picked it up I changed my mind. Although there was no cash in it there were many important-looking papers, including a driver's license and a smattering of personal photos. No, even at my young age I could tell that this was an active wallet, and somebody, somewhere surely must want it back. And so the second thing to come to mind was my moral obligation to perform my civic duty and do my best to return the wallet to its rightful owner. The first thing was: REWARD!

Despite the Internet still being decades away, it was a simple matter, with my parents' help, to track down the owner of the wallet through the phone book. The man was not home, but we left a message with the woman on the other end of the line. We told her we had found his wallet, said he could come by and pick it up that night and we gave her our address. Yes, it certainly was a different time.

To say that the excitement and anticipation I felt that night was comparable to Christmas Eve would be an exaggeration. And it was not visions of sugar plums that danced in my sleepy head, but rather dollar bills; big fat crisp ones. Oh sure, I was truly proud that I had done the responsible thing and contacted the owner, blah, blah, blah, but oh, that delicious reward. Specifically, would there be one and exactly how much could it be?

As I lay in bed I fantasized about the cash windfall that was sure to come my way. How much? How much? Oh sure, a dollar would have been nice and two certainly much appreciated, but what if it was more? What if this stranger was so outrageously happy to get his wallet back, and so incredibly grateful, that be bestowed some incomprehensible sum of money on me? Like, what if he gave me *five* dollars?

Don't scoff so quickly, my friend, at what today seems to you a trifling sum. Remember, this was 1961 and I was eight years old. With five dollars I could go to the movies *seven* times, buy candy for each one of those visits-- Twizzlers or Jawbreakers, please--and have enough left over to purchase the *Meet The Beatles* album, the release date of which was only three short years away. Oh, and I'd still have enough left for another gas station Orange Crush.

And so, lulled by a strangely soothing combination of civic duty and voracious greed, I eventually fell asleep. The next morning my feet hit the floor before my eyes were fully open, and I rushed into the kitchen where my mom was making breakfast. Did he come? I wanted to know. And more importantly, did he pay off? And even *more* importantly, how much?

Unlike a Thanksgiving parade balloon, it took almost no time at all to completely deflate me. Yes, said Mom, the owner of the wallet had come. He had shown up late at night and claimed his wallet. He had clearly been drunk and had not even bothered to say thank you before stumbling back into the dark night and out of our lives forever. And so that was that.

This episode, I would come to learn, while disappointing at the time was not particularly tragic in the grand scheme of things. Despite the lack of a reward, I would still go on to see many movies, consume impressive quantities of candy and eventually even own a copy of *Meet the Beatles*.

I sometimes remember that night of half a century ago and wonder what I would have done had *I* been the parent and my kid had found the wallet. Would I lie and say the drunk was very thankful and hand my kid a five? After all, my parents had lied about Santa Claus to make me happy, so why not this?

I've come to the conclusion that my parents did exactly the right thing. It was a valuable lesson about right and wrong, unrealistic expectations and counting chickens before they hatch. Telling me the truth about what happened that night was not some cynical method employed to teach a young boy to "get used to it" because this is the way the world is. It was a way to show that this is the way the world *sometimes* is. And, more often, is not.

How Damn Long Does It Take to Carve a Mountain Into an Indian?

It's the summer of 1971, I'm eighteen years old and I and my two equally non-svelte brothers are all jammed in the back seat of the family's 1962 Chevy Bel-Air. It's cramped back there and we're fighting for space, as we will continue to do for the next four thousand miles. We are on a family vacation to South Dakota. We're on our way to see Mt. Rushmore.

And, of course, points along the way. There is a sense of adventure in the air; an opportunity for new experience. And the new experiences begin at the Illinois State Fair. Now up until that point my only knowledge of a state fair was through some blurry photos in a school textbook about alien cultures, such as Illinois, and that corny old movie starring Pat Boone. (I'm too young to remember the *really* old one with Dick Haymes.) And now I myself was at my first state fair, complete with cows, sheep and pigs. It was exotic beyond words.

After we had arrived in South Dakota, many uncomfortable miles later, and viewed Mt. Rushmore we learned of another mountain that was being carved right at that very moment. How lucky for us to have arrived during the actual creation of the Crazy Horse Memorial, even if we had almost no idea who Crazy Horse might have been or why somebody would want to carve his image into a stone mountain.

After seeing Mt. Rushmore, the Crazy Horse Memorial was something of a disappointment. Actually, it would have been a disappointment after seeing just about anything. From the viewing platform we looked off into the distance to see a flat rock with a hole cut through it. A mural on a wall told us that the flat part of the rock would be Crazy's extended arm and the hole would be, well, his armpit I suppose. The entire experience reminded me of the episode of *The Flintstones* when they go to see the Grand Canyon and discover only a trickling stream. "They expect it to be a big deal someday," says Fred.

I was not an unromantic kid (all that came later) and as I stood there I looked forward to the day when I would return to see the completed sculpture. In my young mind I estimated that it would probably take about four, and maybe as many as five, years to get the job done. After all, we had read that the guy who was doing the carving was now being assisted by his sons, so I figured that with the whole clan chipping away they'd knock the thing out in no time.

Over the years a photo of the monument under construction would occasionally appear in a newspaper or magazine, and invariably I'd clip the article and send it to my parents or they'd clip it and send it to me. And the only constant in these photos was that Crazy Horse seemed to look exactly the same as he had back in 1971, armpit hole and all. I was sure that there was progress being made, but I'd be damned if I could see it.

And now we are in the computer age and it is a simple matter to keep track of the memorial's progress. A quick trip to Wikipedia reveals a picture of Crazy Horse as he looks today, and damned if he still isn't a big rock with an armpit. OK, to be fair, Crazy Horse now has a face. In fact a dedication ceremony was conducted a few years ago. For the face.

And no doubt there was at least one teenager at that ceremony who looked up at the giant rock with the armpit and made a silent vow: One day soon he would return, perhaps with his own children, to see the finished product.

Keep dreaming, kid.

Foolishness

"Sold!" bellowed the big, jovial man behind the counter as he took my money. "My money" consisted of one dime and one nickel, a not inconsequential amount to a seven year old boy back then. Ah, but so what? I had thought about this investment for quite some time (over an hour!) and now, decision reached, I could barely conceal my excitement as the clerk handed me the treasured purchase.

It was a slice of Swiss cheese, a plastic one. I had chosen it over a counterful of other ingenious novelty and gag items that were featured in the tiny shop just around the corner from my grandmother's house. (I was staying there with my brothers for a week that summer, to have a nice vacation I had thought at the time, but later realized it was to give my parents a much-deserved break.)

I grabbed my faux cheese, thanked the clerk (which is something kids did back then) and rushed out the door of the shop and into my new world; a world, I imagined, where the fun would never stop. Why? Because I now was the owner of a gag that would ensure that my life was about to become nothing short of a string of belly laughs and endless yucks. How could it not?

I raced back to my grandmother's house bursting with giddy anticipation and pride of purchase. You know, I could have spent my dime and nickel on soda or candy. Or both. Back then I could have purchased a soda and a candy bar, or even three full-sized candy bars, for my fifteen cents. But I knew that the rewards of those sugary treats, though delightful, would be short-lived. With the purchase of my fake slice of cheese I was assured that the fun would not last just a few minutes, but for years and years to come.

I couldn't wait to show Grandma my acquisition. And I would show it to her, for although the plan was to slip the cheese into the lunches of my unsuspecting victims, Grandma was not one of my targets. Even at seven I knew that she was one of the nicest people I would ever meet. I could never play a trick on her, no matter how diabolically clever.

What about my crusty old German Grandpa, growling over his lunch in his corner chair by the window? Was it possible that I could slip the bogus cheese into one his headcheese and limburger sandwiches, or whatever the hell he was eating over there? Are you insane? I already mentioned that my plan for the fake food was a life of endless laughs. And clearly part of this plan was to live past my eighth birthday.

"Look, Grandma!" I yelled as I exploded through the front door.

"What is it?" she asked kindly.

I explained that it was a piece of fake Swiss cheese that I had just bought, and I geared up tell her my future plans for big laughs and endless fun, but I was cut short.

"This is foolishness," she said.

Huh?

"This is foolishness," she repeated.

I've thought about this episode over the years and have tried to understand my grandmother's out-of-character and somewhat harsh reaction. I'll never know the reason for sure, but I realized that this was a woman who had struggled through a Great Depression when an extra fifteen cents probably would have meant a lot, and even a slice of cheese, *real* cheese, would have been an unexpected and welcome treat. And here was this little goofball not only being insanely frivolous with his fifteen cents, but worse, spending it on a piece of cheese that you couldn't even eat!

I've just used a savings calculator and found that if fifty years ago I had invested that fifteen cents in the stock market rather than buy that fake cheese my investment today would be worth about $28. And I know now it's what I should have done. Then today I could withdraw that money, go online and purchase that incredibly realistic-looking, premium quality, fake dog poop I've had my eye on. And then I could really have some fun!

313

Oh, now you know that I'm not one for silly superstitions or senseless pseudo-sciences (although some snappy alliteration can still get me hot) but I noticed that my recent expose on the innate stupidity of the horse was essay #313. So what, indeed. Except this number 313 is one that I've been taking notice of regularly and fairly frequently for the past 35 years.

No, it's not a lucky number or a magic number or any of that claptrap. And yet if I happen to see it on a hotel door or as a player's batting average or, God forbid, on a scale that I happen to be standing on, it will always catch my attention. Why? Well, I'll tell you.

Many years ago (and getting many-er every year) in that short sweet time between my friends and I getting our driving licenses and going away to college, Arthur, Howie and I would usually spend Friday and Saturday nights (After I had efficiently dumped off my girlfriend, of course. I guess I really was an a-hole.) driving around talking, listening to music and eventually eating at the local diner. And just for the record we never even consumed so much as a sip of alcohol. You see, dear reader, as difficult as that may be for you to believe, my friends and I were young, had our whole lives ahead of us, and were high on nothing more than life itself. (And the occasional hit of hash oil, but that's a tale for another time.)

One night we were sitting at the diner and someone mentioned that the bill amount was the same as it had been the previous Saturday. That amount of course was $3.13. Then I noticed (Or somebody did. Give me a break. Didn't I tell you this was 35 years ago?) that on the bill there was another 313, as the space labeled "Number of Guests" had a 3 written in and the space next to it contained a 13, which apparently was the number of our table.

Well so far I can tell that you are less than awed by the mild coincidences that have transpired thus far, and the most stunning revelation may well be that three growing high school guys could eat for around three bucks. And so let me warn you that the story does not get any more mind-blowing. But stick around anyway; what else have you got to do?

We left the diner and headed to Howie's house to drop him off. A short time later we were stopped in front of his house and Howie was about to climb out of the car when I (or somebody) said "wouldn't it be amazing if..." and checked his watch. And sure as hell the time was not 3:12 or 3:14 but exactly 3:13. Which today seems amazing to me for two reasons.

First, how did I ever stay up that late? It most certainly would have been around 4:00 when I crawled into bed. Hell, it's not even eleven o'clock right now and I'm nodding off over my keyboard. Oh right , it was 35 years ago.

Second, Arthur, who may be the only person that I've ever admitted *might* actually be smarter than me, was truly spooked by the slight coincidence and insisted on driving once around the block so that we could drop off Howie at a less creepy 3:15. Which we did.

And that's my story. I've lost track of Arthur and Howie, but not of the memory of this strange night from a long time ago. And to this day if a 313 crosses my path it is sure to catch my eye. And if you want to get really freaked out, I just did a word count on this piece and guess what the total number is? Actually it's 647, but still...

The Hot Comb

In the mid-1960's New York Yankee Joe Pepitone took a lot of kidding, and worse, for parading around the locker room wearing a ladies' portable hairdryer. Alas, this was, at that time, the only hair-drying option available to the hirsute Pepitone, short of just letting it dry naturally, as men had done since first crawling out of the sticky primordial ooze.

It wasn't long before the hand-held blow-dryer appeared on the scene and men, women and even tolerant pets could be sporting dry and styled hair minutes after emerging from their shower, bath or stainless steel tub. But before there was the blow-dryer, there was...The Hot Comb.

It wasn't easy having curly hair in the 1960's. The Beatles, after all, had straight hair. And I, like everybody else, also wanted straight hair, but unfortunately the Italian side of the family had cursed me with a rat's nest of brown locks that looked less like Paul McCartney and more like Art Garfunkel. And then one fateful day, while a barber was doing battle with my unruly mane, I spied a box on his shelf containing an alien and somewhat dangerous-looking implement.

"What's that?" I asked the barber.

"That's a hot comb. It straightens hair."

My memory might be a little off here. Looking back, I'm pretty sure the sky didn't actually open up and a chorus of angels descend, singing Alleluia. And yet I knew that my follicle-related prayers had been answered. I immediately bought the not-inexpensive hot comb.

Well, if you've ever seen someone with straightened hair you know that the hot comb didn't transform me into Paul McCartney. But still, it somewhat controlled the Garfunkel look and so I used my hot comb every day. And when it wore out I bought another, and then another after that. And finally the day came when I went away to college. I don't remember if I brought any books with me. I don't remember bringing any pens either, or even any underwear, although I no doubt did. I *do* know that the one thing I didn't forget to pack was my trusty hot comb.

And then one day disaster struck. My hot comb broke. Now back home on Long Island it would have been a simple matter to hop in the car, head to a nearby store and purchase another one. But up the wilds of northern New York State things were different. For one thing I didn't have a car. And for another, we barely had stores. Or at least the type of store that would carry something as frivolous and downright subversive as a hot comb. Hell, I had once been glared at by a snippy clerk who told me, "We don't carry *those* kinds of magazines," when I had asked for a *National Lampoon*.

Panic set in, and I realized that I had two options: I could either face the future with a head of hair that looked like an explosion in a mattress factory or I could attempt to repair the hot comb myself. (Getting a short, sensible haircut was, of course, out of the question. It was 1971.)

And so I found a screwdriver, pried opened the hot comb, reconfigured the wiring and plugged it in.

Nobody ever discovered exactly why the electricity suddenly went out on the entire west wing of my dormitory, nor did anyone smell the faint odor of burning plastic coming from my room. The hot comb at this point was a half-melted and useless appliance that certainly wasn't going anywhere near *my* hair ever again. And so I redoubled my search efforts, and it wasn't long before I found and purchased a brand new hot comb and so could stop wearing the bucket hat I had been using to flatten down my Garfunkeled hairdo.

This happened forty years ago. I no longer resent my curly hair, not even the gray ones. At this point I'm just grateful it chose to stay with me. I happened to see a recent photo of Paul McCartney in a magazine the other day, and I still don't look anything like him. And thank God for that.

Lightning Bugs

Hey, when you were a kid did you used to catch lightning bugs in a jar? I ask because recently I've been wondering if they still even *make* lightning bugs. I know *I* personally haven't seen one in over forty years and was beginning to suspect that perhaps they'd gone the way of the dodo. Or maybe I haven't seen one over the last few decades because their natural flight-path doesn't happen to run between my eyes and my TV screen.

And so, a little research. First I asked my wife if she used to catch lightning bugs (or fireflies, as you might know them) when she was a kid and she said no. So I thought that perhaps this is another of those East Coast/West Coast things, like Hellmann's mayonnaise or White Castle hamburgers. And yet the Internet tells me that lightning bugs are found throughout the world. Ah, but not *everywhere* in the world.

There are over 2,000 species of fireflies, many of which do not produce light, which makes me wonder why they even deserve to be *called* fireflies. (And before your write in with your little corrections, I'll tell you that the larvae of *all* fireflies emit light. They're called glowworms.)

Lightning bugs are a form of beetle, which is something that I didn't know. The light is actually a mating signal, which is absolutely no surprise at all. Heck, just about *everything* in nature is a mating signal.

Many species of lightning bug have a specific flash pattern that helps the amorous little critters locate each other. (Maybe that's part of my problem—perhaps I should start wearing a flashlight around my neck on Ladies Night.)

I found all sorts of scientific mumbo-jumbo about how the light works and what chemical reactions are present in the bug's butt and what wavelength the light is, none of which I'm going to bore you with. It is interesting to note that the ancient Chinese sometimes captured a bunch of lightning bugs in transparent containers and used these as primitive (and short lived) lanterns. *That's* kind of cool to know, I suppose.

You see, all I know about lightning bugs is the memory of warm summer nights when the neighborhood kids would run around (or stand ve-r-r-ry still) in the backyard, clutching a glass jar in one hand and the lid in the other, waiting to spot that telltale blink of light in the darkness. And then, with the distinctive sound of metal hitting glass, the jar was slammed closed and maybe, just maybe, you had captured a lightning bug. And when you finally did you put the glowing jar on the table next to your bed and watched that bug cast a soft glow in your room long into the night, or at least until sleep overtook you.

And the next morning, despite the air holes you poked into the jar's lid and despite the blades of grass you gave your new pet to munch on, your lightning bug would most likely be dead. What the heck--you were only seven years old. It would be a decade or two at least before you would come to realize that lightning bugs, like most things in nature, were meant to be looked at, appreciated and left alone.

Spring 1959

It's still gray, which doesn't really surprise me. It was also gray back then and, as far as I know, it has always been gray. I have no idea why it has always been painted the same color, but it gives me a sense of comfort, of continuity, and that makes me happy.

It seemed a big, old house back then, and it still does as I imagine myself on the sidewalk out front. This is the same sidewalk that I walked on many mornings on my way to kindergarten, and where I first learned to ride a two-wheeler. And where I first fell off that two-wheeler. It's not how often you fall, it's how many times you get back up, goes the old cliché. Could anything ever be more true?

I head up the walkway and climb the three or four steps of the brick porch, or "stoop" as we would have called it. I feel the short climb in my knees and pause to catch my breath as I approach the front door. I reach for the knob but immediately stop. This is as far as I can go. For inside the house it is 1959 and I am of 2013, and I would not be understood or welcome.

It seems that nearly every window on the large gray house is open, and I can hear the radio inside, although I am not quite sure what music is playing. Perhaps it is Lloyd Price singing his hit "Personality," a song I was once urged to sing for a group of my mother's friends. The group, all girls in their twenties I realize now, had clapped enthusiastically. At the time I had thought they were recognizing an immensely talented six-year-old, not aware that they had simply thought I was cute.

But it wasn't the radio playing, it was my mother singing. The windows of the house were open because it was spring cleaning day, and my mom armed with a bottle of Windex (glass, not plastic) was singing as she went about what still seems to me a Herculean and disagreeable task. I inherited many traits from my mother, including a mop of uncontrollable hair and an independent streak bordering on stubbornness, but the ability to sing merrily while working was, sadly, not one of them. I tend, instead, to grumble.

Inside, the six year old boy sits at the kitchen table and colors. He appears to be quiet and calm, but his mind is racing. And why not? So much to see, so much to think about. Today he feels good. The breeze, created by the open windows and sweeping through the house, is almost brisk, but not quite. The house, the entire world, seems fresh and clean and new, and it feels wonderful. Still, he doesn't know that he'll always remember this day.

Through the kitchen window he spies a robin, and he is ecstatic. He knows there is something special about seeing this first robin of spring, though he is not sure exactly what. Does he win a prize for the sighting? Is there some sort of magic involved? It would be years, decades, before he realizes that yes, there was indeed magic there.

My father is off at work protecting his assigned plot of New York City and my younger brothers are nowhere to be found. I know they must have been around, seeing how they were but four and one at the time. But this is *my* memory and, though they will star in many others, this one features just me and my mom.

The boy gives the robin one more look and then returns to his coloring. He listens to the "squeak-squeak-squeak" as his mother wipes another window clean with her Windex and rags. She continues to sing and although the boy does not know the songs by name he has heard them before. Years later he will identify two of them as "Que Sera Sera" and "Scarlet Ribbons" and think, as the Rolling Stones blast from his stereo, that his mother's songs are the corniest things he has ever heard. And then, many years after that, he will come to believe that they are precious.

Sew What?

It's a timeless image: a young woman sitting in chair sewing the material she has draped across her lap. In this case the young woman was one of those hard-bodied aqua-nazis who each week makes sure I don't drown as I drag my middle-aged carcass from one side of the pool to the other. And the object she is sewing is not a pair of her husband's pants or a jumper for her toddler, but rather a rubber wetsuit in need of repair. But still, it's a scene that still evokes images of long ago, of a pioneer woman, or perhaps a woman sitting in the glow of a radio dial, trying to make do with what she has. And it caused me to wonder: do women still sew?

My grandmother had an antique sewing machine. Oh, it wasn't antique when she had it but it would certainly qualify today. So would Grandma, now that I think of it. It didn't run on electricity but rather was powered by a foot pedal underneath it. It seems that sewing was a pretty big thing back then. Not only did Grandma own a fairly intricate, and probably expensive, sewing machine but she kept it and used it in a sewing room. That is, a room dedicated specifically and exclusively to sewing. And for getting away from Grandpa, no doubt.

My mother also had a Singer sewing machine. (I'd say we were a loyal Singer family but then again what other sewing machine company is there? Does the Federal Trade Commission know about this monopoly?) But unlike Grandma's sewing machine, Mom's used electricity. It was operated by a sickle-shape piece of metal that she pushed with her right knee to get the needle to go up and down.

I recall the sewing machine was not some piece of apparatus like a pasta maker or a ThighMaster--purchased, used a couple of times and then thrown into a closet to corrode into a pile of useless scrap metal. No, Mom used that sewing machine a *lot*. Socks, pants, shirts--they all got repaired to be worn another day. Hell, if the needle had been strong enough she probably would have used it to re-attach those hanging shoe soles that made that annoying tell-tale sound, announcing our poverty as it flopped noisily when we walked down the street.

My wife Spike does not own a sewing machine. In fact she does not own a needle and thread. There are rumors that Spike knows how to crochet, but I've seen precious little evidence of it over the last twenty years. I myself keep one of those travel sewing kits in my underwear drawer for emergencies. It sees the light of day perhaps twice a year, when a seam bursts on a relatively new shirt or when I need a needle to lance a blister. There was a time when a woman might spend an entire evening "darning" her family's holey socks. Now the socks get thrown into the trash at the first sign of wear. Hey, why make the effort when you can get six pair for $4.99 at Wal-Mart?

Still, there was something eternal about that young woman sewing at the pool last week. For a moment I toyed with the idea of asking her, as a joke, if next week I could bring a few of my worn socks for her to stitch up. But I didn't. It is, after all, the 21st century. And besides, I didn't want to give her a reason, if the opportunity should arise, to just let me drown.

Sal, Sal, The Ice Cream Pal

I just got an e-mail from my lifelong chum Lenny and in it he mentioned Sal, who was the guy who used to drive his ice cream truck around our Long Island neighborhood when we were kids in the early 1960's. That I still remember Sal, when I have forgotten books I've read, friends I've laughed with and lovers I've loved, says volumes about his promotional skills, as well as the nutritional habits of the childhood me.

It's hard to say exactly how old Sal the Ice Cream Man was. Back then to a pre-teen anybody over the age of thirty was an absolute antique, and it depresses me to admit that I'm sure this attitude hasn't much changed, even among today's hip-hop pimple poppers. My guess is that Sal was somewhere between the ages of thirty and fifty, and really how could a man who chose driving an ice cream truck not as a summer job but as a vocation be anything but?

The thing is Sal had gray hair, but looking at the image of him in my head, always smiling, always hustling, I think he was what we would call prematurely gray. The joke among us kids at the time was that his hair turned gray because his head spent so much time getting ice cream out of the freezers. Hey, I suppose you think *you* were wittier at ten?

If you haven't figured it out by now, Sal had a style. He sold ice cream with an enthusiasm and verve that made the other ice cream vendors seem tired and old by comparison. We even had a little jingle that we created for him. "Sal, Sal, the ice cream pal," we would sing. It never was a hit, but has anyone ever written a jingle about you? Me neither. (A restraining order, yes, but not a jingle.)

You can talk about Donald Trump or Bill Gates, but compared to Sal they're mere slackers. Sal the Ice Cream Man was a true marketing mastermind. On some days Sal would arrive after the Mr. Softee truck or the Good Humor truck was long gone but still, as eager as we were to get that ice cream, we waited for Sal.

"Don't buy from them others, always wait for your pal, Sal," I remember him saying one day, whispering it as if he was being investigated by the government for anti-trust violations in his ice cream practices. And if you *didn't* wait for him you felt guilty as hell. Sal was a genius.

And so wait we did. And besides, what other ice cream vendor gave you the opportunity to earn a free ice cream? Did you hear what I just said? *Free ice cream!* You see, whenever you made a purchase from Sal he would give you a little plastic charm. Once you accumulated ten of these charms you would get yourself a free ten-cent ice cream, which in truth was probably more of an ice treat, such as a popsicle. Now if you could hold on until you collected *fifteen* of the charms, and trust me it wasn't easy (those charms burned a hole in your pocket clean and true) then you could get the good stuff: chocolate-dipped pops, sprinkled cones and, yum, goopy sundaes.

Every summer some evil-minded kid (who is now probably an evil-minded multi-millionaire) would suggest that we go to the store and buy a big bag of those charms and then get all the free ice cream we could eat. But we kids would never do such a thing; for one thing it was dishonest and for another, it was Sal.

When last heard from years ago the rumor was that Sal had retired and moved to Florida. If this is true then perhaps my estimates about his age were way off and he actually had been well over fifty. On the other hand maybe he was simply a prematurely gray and enterprising young man who got rich and retired early by using his charm, and his charms, to cleverly and uncompromisingly corner the much-coveted ice cream market on Windhorst Avenue.

The Hippie Chick: Part I – I Win the Lottery

She was a hippie chick and as such she sported the accepted regalia of the time: sandals, worn jeans with assorted dove and peace symbol patches, various leather-strapped necklaces, a white peasant blouse and no bra.

She had just risen from the cushion on which she had been sitting, the only girl among the nine or ten college students crammed into the smoky dorm room, and was heading my way. This in response to my having just poked my head through the doorway and asking, "Any news yet?"

It was February 2, 1972, the day of the military draft lottery. All over the country anxious nineteen year old men -- boys -- gathered around radios to listen to the results. To hear their fate. The country was "at war," as usual, and each year a lottery was held to decide which, and in what the order, the young men would be drafted into the armed forces. For each day of the year a number from 1 – 366 was randomly drawn. Your place in line was determined by the number that was paired with your birthday.

I, like everyone else, wanted a high number—the bigger the better. Finding out that something over 300 would be posted next to January 6th would have been the sweetest of dreams. But the genuinely sad look in the hippie chick's eyes told me that it was a dream that was not meant to be.

As she gently grabbed my arm and walked me down the dormitory hallway I began to babble nervously, to make jokes where no humor was called for. "Did I win? Am I Number One! Oooh, I hope so! I never won anything before!" The hippie chick wasn't buying it for a second. She maintained her serious yet sympathetic expression and informed me that my number was 26, a number so low that in most, if not all, previous years it had been as good as an express ticket to Vietnam.

The entire scenario was unimaginable to me. Me in the army? I was a college student! I liked books and movies and marijuana. I don't even kill spiders. Why, I had never even fired a gun! (I still haven't.)

The Hippie Chick: Part II – Pretzels in the Woods

Several months later I was summoned to take an army physical in Albany, New York, about a two-hour bus ride from my school. I remember two things about that day. First, that when they took my sitting pulse rate it clocked in at a hyper 108 beats per minute. I was later informed that I would have to return for another physical, this time spending the night at a local hotel. They wanted to keep an eye on me. It was not uncommon at the time for a young man to ingest any manner of drug to help him fail his physical, say for having a heart rate of 108.

But I hadn't taken anything, partly because I wouldn't do that and partly because I didn't know how. What do you take and where do you get it? If you couldn't roll it into a joint or stuff it into a bong I was out of my league. Had they asked I could have told them that the only medical problem I was suffering from was what I would later refer to as The Scared Shitless Syndrome.

The second thing I remember from that day was being lined up with a group of my fellow teenagers. We might have been fully clothed, but it was more likely that we were in our underwear. The man in charge barked at us to do a single push-up, which we all did. It was my first military command, and I resented the fuck out of it.

That Christmas, around the dinner table, my uncle teased me about my impending military service. "Next

Christmas you'll be eating pretzels in the woods!" Whether this image came from one of his own delightful memories of his time with the Russian army I never knew. I just knew that I failed to see the humor in his kidding. In fact, it scared the hell out of me. (Despite my liking both pretzels *and* the woods.)

I was never called back for my follow-up physical. The war was winding down and the draft would soon be ending. Mom recently reminded me about how happy I was when I got the letter from Selective Service telling me I would not be drafted. I'm sure I was relieved to see it in print, but I believe it had been common knowledge months earlier that few numbers, if any, would be called from that year's lottery. They wouldn't even get to 26.

But, ah, that hippie chick. I don't remember her name, her face or even what she was doing in the freshmen men's dorm that day. Yet I'll always remember her act of kindness on that terrible day over four decades ago. I hope she's having a peaceful, loving and groovy life.

Responsible Lieutenant Leonard

It was a dark and rainy morning, but that didn't matter; I was at my post. And why wouldn't I be? As a lieutenant on the Safety Patrol I had taken on a responsibility and I was not about to let a touch of inclement weather get in my way.

I wish I could have said the same for the *other* three Safety Patrollers who were supposed to be on duty with me, standing guard around the periphery of the parking lot, protecting our civilian classmates as they made their way to begin another day of school.

But no, I was the only one who bothered to show up on that stormy day. The others, I assumed, has chosen to spend a few extra minutes in the warmth of their beds. Slackers! (Or whatever it was that we called such shirkers back in 1964.)

After I had fulfilled my duty, and only then, did I allow myself to enter the brightness and warmth of the school. I went about my day doing all the things that were required of me, as well as taking the time to report to Mr. Ross, the Safety Patrol faculty advisor, that I had indeed been the *only* one at his post that morning.

After school I attended the regularly scheduled Safety Patrol meeting where Mr. Ross gave an energetic and high-volumed lecture about responsibility. "Leonard here was the only one of you who showed up at his post this morning. He knows what it means to be responsible," he said at one point. .

Normally I would have beamed with pride at the praise but I had other things on my mind. I knew that when the meeting ended I would once again have to report an unpleasant fact to Mr. Ross. A few minutes later, and for the second time that day, I approached Mr. Ross.

"Mr. Ross?" I said sheepishly.

"Yes, Leonard?" Mr. Ross answered, instantly bestowing one of his rare 100-watt smiles on his star lieutenant.

"Uh, I, uh lost my Safety Patrol badge and belt today."

The smile faded immediately, and I knew what Mr. Ross was thinking. I knew because he couldn't resist also saying it aloud:

"You lost your badge? On the same day I gave a speech about how responsible you are?" He gave a little humorless smile and I saw that he had recognized the irony of the situation. I also knew that I would now forever be the butt of a story with which he would regale his friends over glasses of wine and at dinners for many, many years to come.

Tales of Unspeakable Woe: New Year's Eve

In most ways it was a typical New Year's Eve for my brothers and me. Mom and Dad had gone to a party "down the street," but not before leaving their growing boys an assortment of chips, dip, soda and other assorted party food that would supply the empty calories so necessary to help see us into the new year.One of the thrills of New Year's Eve was that we were allowed to pull the largest of the pots and pans from the cabinet under the stove, find the biggest metal spoons from the nearby utensil drawer and create as much of a racket as we wanted, dents and sleeping neighbors be damned. In truth this demonstration was, and had always been, more exciting for my two younger brothers than it ever was for me. Excepting maybe an amped-up concert by the Who or the unrestrained screams of a woman in ecstasy, I never much cared for loud noises.

And yet as typical as this New Year's was, it was in some ways so very different. I was fifteen years old now, and spending this supposed bacchanalian holiday with my two little brothers was becoming less and less enthralling with each passing year. In truth, at fifteen, with a torrent of fresh raw hormones surging through my body, I didn't want to spend New Year's Eve banging pots and pans. I wanted to spend it banging Janie.

Not that I actually knew what that meant back then. I just had some vague notion that this was supposed to be one of the most romantic nights of the year, and I should-- and wanted to--spend it with Janie.

Janie, by the way, was not actually my girlfriend. We did have an unspoken attraction towards each other, and had since we'd discovered each other in fourth grade. In eighth grade Janie had been my first official "date," as we'd walked a mile together on a crisp winter evening to go to Confession. But it was now three years later and my idea of a perfect date had little, if anything, to do with religion. Not that we had even so much as kissed or held hands at this point. We hadn't.

It's to my credit, I suppose, that I was actually feeling sorrier for Janie on that New Year's Eve than I was for myself. As the clock approached midnight and my brothers guzzled soda and inhaled chips as if awaiting execution, the image of a sad and lonely Janie grew clearer and clearer in my mind. I pictured her all alone, sitting by a silent phone and willing it to ring, a ring that would never come. It was shameful that Janie, this young and beautiful girl, was all by herself on New Year's Eve, and I couldn't help but think that it was all my fault.

The feeling started in the pit of my stomach, a peculiar mixture of courage and nausea. By 11:45 the courage was, uncharacteristically, gaining control, and I knew what I had to do. I reached for the telephone and dialed Janie's number. This task was made more difficult by the nosiness of my brothers who were suddenly and for the first time distracted from their high-caloric feast.

Who are you calling? my siblings wanted to know, and I told them it was none of their business. I was already resigned to the fact that there would be, of course, little to no privacy. This was 1968, after all, and the family phone, like most family phones, was firmly and permanently fixed to the wall. And so before I even dialed the seventh digit of Janie's number (which of course, I knew for memory) the inevitable chant began: "Lenny's got a girlfriend! Lenny's got a girlfriend!"

I stretched the telephone's springy spiral cord to its limit and, with beads of stress-sweat starting to form on my forehead, found a dark quiet corner in the dining room just as I heard Janie's voice. She *was* home! I knew it!

"Hello?" she said hesitantly.

"Hello, Janie. It's Lenny. I just called to wish you--"

"Hello? Hello?"

Although my brothers had lost interest in my amorous escapades and mercifully quieted down, I was still having trouble hearing Janie, and she me. Eventually she must have found her own quiet and dark corner and we exchanged a few words. But it no longer much mattered. You see, my image of saving Janie from her sad, lonely New Year's Eve was vaporizing quicker than a glob of spit on a sizzling summer sidewalk. The reason I was having so much trouble hearing her was because Janie, the love of my short life and just a few blocks away, was having a New Year's Eve party. It sounded like it was fun, too. I wished her a Happy New Year and hung up the phone.

Later that week I saw Janie in school and she explained that the reason she couldn't invite me to her party was because her "New York City Boyfriend" was there. I suspect she told me this with the intention of somehow making me feel better. It didn't.

Old, Old Stuff

After years of thinking about it I finally took all my dusty treasures that had been stashed in the rapidly disintegrating cardboard box labeled "old, old stuff" and transferred them into a shiny new state-of-the-art plastic storage container, with patented locking lid. And then I labeled *that* "old, old stuff."

Not that all of the junk in that box was particularly ancient. In fact most of it only goes back as far as my childhood, and I'll thank you to keep your snide comments to yourself. I rummaged around and found some baseball cards, mostly of players you've never heard of, and an autographed baseball which includes the signature of Yogi Berra. There were some slides of a camping trip taken in 1965 and even a class photo from third grade. Gosh, I was a cute kid.

Actually there *were* some old, old things in the box. There was a Bible from 1634 and some newspapers telling of a presidential assassination. No, not Kennedy. Lincoln. There was a bullet from the Battle of Gettysburg and a hand-written and decorated book page from around 1220. That's pretty old, eh?

I like old objects--I've always been fascinated by these physical links to the past. I remember sitting in the guidance counselor's office in eighth grade and answering his question with a chirpy, "An archeologist!" The poor man was at a loss, which I didn't understand at the time, and so I watched curiously as he fumbled helplessly through his rack of Accountant, Nurse and Teacher brochures.

I caught a bit of *Antiques Roadshow* tonight and I suddenly realized that my perspective has changed. As I'm getting older I'm starting to see the "big picture." Up until fairly recently I had always looked at these old bits of stuff as objects that had worked their way down through the years, following a long and winding road until settling in their final resting place which, of course, was with me. Here now we have one more example of thinking that I can put in my ever-expanding file that I've labeled "The Arrogance of Youth."

When I was given my antique Bible and Lincoln newspaper by my great-great-aunt I had foolishly assumed that they were now mine. And it's taken me nearly forty years to realize that I'll be doing nothing more than simply holding them for a while. And then the Bible, the newspapers and all my other accumulated stuff will continue on their journey through time, like a leaf floating down a stream. And without me.

And I also begin to realize that older people understand this, and so begin to give away their treasured possessions to those they care about, in order to help both the stuff and the person on their way. I can see the time approaching where I too will begin to bestow my most valued possessions upon my most valued people. But that won't be for quite a while yet. So don't even *think* about asking for the Yogi Berra ball.

My First Cussin'

You think you had it rough? Try being a curly-haired boy growing up during the Beatles Era. I tell you, I've known *real* pain. And it was this pain that on one particular day in 1964 caused me to utter my first curse word. Yes, I may not remember what I had for breakfast but I sure as hell know when I said my first obscenity.

I would have killed for a Beatle haircut at the time, but even then I knew it was never going to happen. My locks, if allowed to grow, were and always would be more of the Art Garfunkel variety. I was still combing my hair with the wave in front, and I was still frustrated by one little curl that refused to stay in place. It never failed—five minutes after I emerged from the boys' room with damp hair plastered into place the errant follicles would curl around to form a near-perfect loop. And I hated it.

On this day my fifth grade teacher Mr. Z had asked me to deliver a message to Mrs. B., who had been my fourth grade teacher. Now as a teacher Mrs. B. had been a bit of a hard-ass and escaping her class to Mr. Z.'s was like being released on parole. I'm tempted to further describe her as an old, old lady but you remember how that goes: It may be that Mrs. B. was at the time younger than I am right now. So let's just say that I *believe* that Mrs. B. was a decaying old fossil, but I wouldn't bet my life on it. Yours yes, but not mine.

Mrs. B. didn't have to say anything more than a simple thank you when I delivered the message. And I would have returned to Mr. Z.'s class with my verbal purity still intact. But no, Mrs. B. had to open her wizened mouth and make a comment. It was a question actually, and this is what she asked:

"How long did it take you to make that curl?"

I didn't explode. And if you're thinking that I cursed at her you're way off. I was furious, yes, but I wasn't an idiot. I answered her question with some sort of joke and walked down the hallway to return to my classroom. And just because the steam that was coming out of my ears wasn't visible to Mrs. B., myself or anybody who happened to be in the hall doesn't mean it wasn't there.

As angry as I was I cannot deny that vocalizing the curse word was calculated. I waited until I was far enough away from Mrs. B. to be out of earshot. I looked up and down the hallway, and then I muttered under my breath, "Damn her."

I don't think it felt particularly good or bad to finally use an expletive out loud. It was simply time to do it, and a relief to get it over with. It was, in a way, much like losing my virginity. But unfortunately *that* particular rite of passage took a lot longer to accomplish, and with a lot more effort. And it's a story for another day.

ADDENDUM: I lied to you. This was actually the *second* time in my life that I had used a curse word. It was, however, the first time I did it consciously and also the first occurrence that I remember. There is a delightful family story that I must share. According to my parents, when I was about two I was in the playpen trying to climb out. My parents, curious if I could actually do it, kept encouraging me. Finally, bursting with infantile frustration and resignation, I yelled out, "I can't do it, goddammit!"

I was such a special child.

Mexican Hats

It seems like a very strange experience for a nine year old boy to have, even an odd little fellow like myself. My fourth grade class had gone on a field trip to see a popular new movie. The year was 1962 and the film was *How the West Was Won.*

I remember that I had been assigned a less than ideal seat, way off on the left side of the theater, and that my snack of choice that day was a gooey, dentist-condemned candy called Mexican Hats. I'm not sure if they still make this confection, what with political correctness and all, but I know that I only bought them as a rather poor substitute for my favorite at the time. The theater, to their everlasting shame, did not carry Jujyfruits.

What I remember most about that day was the unexpected and deep feeling of melancholia that came over me somewhere during the movie. I suddenly, and apparently without reason, became very sad at the realization that one day my mother would die. For years I thought that it was a very peculiar thing for a nine year old boy to be thinking about. And I especially wondered why this feeling would manifest while I watched a movie, and an overblown western epic at that. In Cinerama!

Just a few weeks ago I watched a part of *How the West Was Won* on television. I was struck by one scene between a mother and her young son, as the son was preparing to go off and fight in the Civil War. The poor old mom was played by Carroll Baker. The actress was thirty at the time.

It's a powerful and touching scene, and I now wondered if it had perhaps been the catalyst for that feeling of sadness that overwhelmed that nine year old boy as he sat in the dark chomping on his Mexican Hats. Maybe, but I can never really know for sure.

And now the inevitable has come to pass and my mother has died. That distant yet familiar sadness has found me again, this time with a vengeance. If I had a time machine I would go back and tell that nine year old boy to relax and enjoy his movie and his Mexican Hats. He would have his mom around for the next forty-eight years. What I wouldn't tell him is that he'd someday feel as if those forty-eight years had passed in the blink of an eye.

Memories of Shea

Here's another way to gauge if perhaps you are becoming a bit long in the tooth: when they tear down a stadium that you can remember being built.

My dad sent me an article that named the top ten moments in the history of Shea Stadium. The greatest moment is Bill Buckner's infamously booted ground ball in game six of the 1986 World Series. Number Three on the list is the Beatles 1965 concert and Number Eight is the visit of John Paul II in front of a crowd of 60,000. Call me a heathen, but I'm thrilled that the Beatles beat out the Pope. They wrote much better songs, and had cooler haircuts besides.

Four of the top ten moments took place over a sixteen-month period. They included two games during the Miracle Mets' 1969 season, Joe Namath's "Heidi Game" from the year before and one stunning pitching performance by Tom Seaver the year after. I too have some fond, and not so fond, memories of Shea Stadium.

It wasn't an easy task to get from Bethpage to Flushing. You had to take the Long Island Railroad and you had to switch trains, a tricky and even dangerous maneuver. The adults told us we were crazy when, at the age of fourteen, my childhood chum Lenny and I said we were going to a ballgame by ourselves. They laughed at a lot of things we said we were going to do, but we did them anyway.

The only thing more difficult than getting to Shea in those days was staying there and watching another miserable performance by the New York Mets. From their inception in 1962 through 1968 the Mets never had a winning season. And they never finished higher than ninth place in the ten-team National League. Still, we went and cheered for the hapless losers, usually on a Sunday when teams almost always played a double-header.

My earliest memories of Shea include sitting through two games, often in the rain. Usually the Mets had lost the first game and were being thoroughly trounced in the second when we snuck down from our cheap seats to the now-empty box seats we could never hope to afford. By then it was the eighth inning, the Mets was losing by ten or more and nobody, least of all the security guards, gave a damn where we sat.

And so, despite the fate of our wretched team, we allowed ourselves to temporarily enjoy the magical view. Soon the second game was also lost and we filed out amidst the memorable and not entirely unpleasant stench that can only be created by just the right combination of misty rain, spilled beer, soggy newspapers, squished hot dogs and dirty, dirty New York City air.

1969 changed everything. It was during this enchanted season that I got to witness what Tom Seaver himself has called the greatest game he ever pitched. No, it didn't make the top ten list, but me and Tom were both there on that July 9th and we know. Seaver had been masterful and was within two outs of pitching a perfect game when a punk named Jimmy Qualls, just up from the minors, hit a clean single and ruined the night for Seaver, me and 60,000 other fans. As you can no doubt tell, I'm still a little pissed off at this Qualls guy.

It was just a little over two months later when I leaped onto the field and into the arms of my deliriously and equally happy friend Arthur. This was not typical behavior for sixteen year old boys, but then again this was not a typical night. The New York Mets, on their way to becoming the Miracle Mets, had just clinched first place for the first time ever, and our joy was boundless. And I, right in the middle of all the yelling, cheering and yes, love, reached down and shyly pulled a few blades of grass from the field.

So now they've knocked down Shea Stadium. They ripped out the box seats and plowed up that hallowed lawn, but that's fine. You see, they can't tear down all those happy memories. And yes, I still have those blades of grass.

I Remember Daniel Brown

When I awoke this morning the only dream I could recall involved two older, but not unattractive, women who were trying to coerce me into returning with them to their apartment. I suppose the fact that they were both older than I and yet neither used a walker was also memorable, but whether I took them up on the offer I can't say. In addition to this dream snippet I also found myself waking up with the memory of Daniel Brown in my head.

In case you're new to my writing, let me tell you I have a head stuffed with useless information, obscure facts interesting only to me and endless memories, happy and otherwise, from long ago. I can remember the names of every one of my elementary school teachers, including the two women who taught my kindergarten class: Miss Weissglass and Miss Glasner. I even remember quipping to them that we had "two glasses" teaching our class. Hey give me a break, I was only five. Besides I still contend that my "glass" comment is no less funny than Lou Costello's "We have a couple of 'days' on the team," and millions roared at that.

And while I *do* remember many of my classmates from second grade I do not remember a single one from first grade. And yet, oddly, I remember one, and only one, of my fellow students from kindergarten. His name was Daniel Brown.

No, he was not a friend. I suppose at some point during the year we might have spoken to each other (although I'm not sure that kids in kindergarten in the 1950's were even *allowed* to speak) but if we did I don't recall it. In fact I only remember Daniel Brown for a single incident, one which, I must tell you with equal parts of embarrassment and awe, happened almost exactly half a century ago.

Let me be honest and admit that I'm filling in some of the gaps here, but as best as I can recollect a group of students were seated around a large table, which was actually made up of four desks that had been pushed together. I don't remember what activity we had been involved with, probably making misshapen mooses out of construction paper or some other bullshit project that was specifically designed to keep us out of our parents' hair for six hours.

The "fun" had come to an end, and one of the Glasses instructed us to clean up the floor underneath our desks. Like the good little boy I was, and continue to be, I immediately dropped to the floor and began to pick up the tiny bits of colored paper that were the jetsam of the moose project. And while on the floor I glanced over at the kids on the other side and couldn't believe what I saw.

There was Daniel Brown, a pudgy, curly-haired kid (and who wasn't?) on his hands and knees. But Daniel Brown was not picking up the tiny pieces of paper like the rest of us. Daniel Brown had his palm spread open on the floor and was *brushing the paper and other bits of debris over to my section of the floor!*

I have no other memory of this event except that I know I felt a white-hot sense of outrage by the unfairness of what Daniel Brown was doing. This morning I was still congratulating myself for at least not snitching on the fat little bastard, but after more thought I cannot absolutely swear that I didn't. Those files, I'm afraid, are permanently erased.

I'm a big believer that the traits exhibited in children will often be with them for the rest of their lives, and I think you'll find that science will back me up on this. For example, although I never would have committed a crime as heinous as Daniel Brown's, there is also no way I can guarantee you that I didn't use the opportunity of being under the desks to sneak a peek up a dress or two. I don't remember doing it, but I can't promise that I didn't.

I occasionally wonder whatever happened to Daniel Brown. I firmly believe that anyone capable of such a deceitful and self-centered action, and at such an early age, has no doubt become outrageously successful in life, but as what? So Daniel Brown, if you're out there reading this drop me a line and let me know in what field you achieved your monumental success. I'm guessing you're a lawyer.

Frank at the Bat

We had won the game. I was as sure of it as I would ever be of anything, ever. The bases were loaded and my team was ahead by one run in the bottom of the ninth with two outs. You wonder how, looking into home from my right field position, I could be so confident that the win was in the bag. After all, having the opposing team load up the bases in the bottom of the ninth while your team held onto the slimmest of leads was one of the most tenuous, sphincter-clenching situations in baseball. How could I be so positive that we were about a minute and a half from victory? Easy. Frank was up.

Frank was, without a doubt, the worst player ever to jam a glove onto the wrong hand and trip over a foul line as he stumbled his way out to his position in left field. Remember the worst player on the team when you were a kid? He was Jeter compared to Frank. Frank couldn't catch, he couldn't throw and even his attempts to run were a fifty-fifty proposition that he'd fall on his face before reaching his destination. Which, incidentally, was never first base. Why? Because Frank would strike *out every single time* he was at the plate.

Then why was Frank batting in this crucial game situation? The answer was simple: it was his turn. As kids we played many variations of the grand old game, from the exceedingly rare nine-men-on-a-side purist version to a bastardized street interpretation with but two men on each team, parallel baselines and invisible men on the bases. Sure, this might have made old Abner Doubleday spin a time or two, but what could you do? The nature of the day's game was defined by the number of kids available to play.

And this particular day was a rarity in the extreme. Somehow four, five, six small groups of friends from diverse neighborhoods had converged on a literal sandlot and the game was played with the full nine men on a side. Not everybody knew each other, but we knew that, outside of organized ball, a game like this, played the way baseball was meant to be played, was not likely to occur again in our fleeting childhoods.

When I look back at this game, and several other games where Frank was present, I always marvel at the democracy, fairness and sheer decency of it. I'm not sure why Frank was allowed to play, for whichever team took him would without a doubt be handicapped by getting only two outs every three innings or so. Frank was what was known as an "automatic out." If fact, he was the very definition of it. And yet to those dozen and a half boys the very concept of "being allowed to play" was as alien to them as a laptop computer with instant pornography would have been. Frank was there, he had a glove and he wanted to play. And so he played. Just not very well.

Which takes us back to that summer day, and that long-ago game. I knew that I could have sat in the grass while I waited for Frank to take his three mandatory swings. Hell, I could have even pulled out a comic book. But I didn't do either of these things, or anything else except lean over with my hands on my knees and watch the batter. To do otherwise would have been rude. There's no sitting in baseball. And so I stood, ever ready for the fly ball that I knew, at least in this case, would and could never come.

After the game we went off to a local deli to buy soda, candy and other sugar-based comestibles to help us celebrate our one-run victory. What, did you think we lost? Did you think that Frank had somehow managed to make himself the unlikely hero with a perfectly placed single or even a dramatic game-ending grand slam? Hey, this was real life, not some treacly Afterschool Special. Didn't you even bother to read the second paragraph? Of course Frank struck out. Frank *always* struck out. But he always played.

Fairy Hooks

Does anybody but me remember fairy hooks? I'm going to resist the easy, crude humor here, probably perhaps for the first time since I started writing, and tell you that when we were kids fairy hooks are what we called those little cloth loops that were on the back of many men's dress shirts.

I heard a reference to them the other day on an old *Mystery Science Theater* episode, except the term used was " fruit loops." In either case there seemed to be an implication back then that any male who happened to have one of these short pieces of cloth sewn onto his shirt was somehow lacking in masculinity. At least that's what these names implied.

Despite the names, however, I don't recall any guys being ridiculed or ostracized for having fairy hooks on their shirts, as they most certainly would have been for other, more unforgivable crimes, such as sitting near the front of the bus or carrying a school bag. In fact, there was a time when I was in the fifth when having a fairy hook on your shirt was a great way to attract the ladies. Are you sure nobody else out there remembers all this?

For a brief time it became the style for young girls to collect these fairy hooks. I still recall the image of a small ten-year-old girl's sweaty fist as it clutched a handful of about a dozen of these things, although I can't seem to recall exactly to whom that fist was attached.

There were basically two ways for a girl to obtain her fairy hook trophy. By far the most common was to ask the boy if she could have his fairy hook, and then gently pull it off the shirt or even snip it with a pair of scissors. Then there was the *other* way.

I believe her name was Bernadette—a precocious little fifth-grader who wore make-up and sported one of our class's first sets of budding breasts. The victim, and I know you're surprised that it wasn't me, was a slow-witted fellow named Mark.

It must have happened during a particularly frenetic day of fairy hook hunting. In fact, I don't think I actually saw the attack. I only remember the aftermath: our teacher sternly lecturing the class as Bernadette sat sheepishly at her desk while Mark sat at his, looking quite downcast due in no small part to the giant rip down the back of his shirt. And thus began the decline in popularity of The Great Fairy Hook Fad of 1965.

I think I felt sorry for Mark on that day, but my pity evaporated seven years later when this same half-wit spent hours attempting to bed my girlfriend while I was 300 miles away at college. (Where I was no doubt trying to bed someone else, but still...)

And as for Bernadette, who can say whatever became of her? Maybe she became a seamstress, or used her early aggressiveness to smash through the glass ceiling and rise to the top of the business world. Or maybe she never quite recovered from that teacher-induced humiliation inflicted on her all those years ago, and today sits on the floor of her institutional room, wearing pajamas and a robe, and humming quietly to herself while she twists and turns that little strip of cloth in her hands for days at a time.

Whitey Ford is Nicer Than Me

We'll have to again set the Way-Back Machine for tonight's entry. Let's take it back to about 1964, when some kids from our block were taken to the Bronx by our fathers to watch a Yankee game. I don't remember how many kids went, or exactly who they were. They were all kids from our neighborhood, but I'm not going pretend that I remember each and every individual from that night so long ago. After all, unlike Whitey Ford, I'm not a liar.

A little background: Whitey Ford was a pitching star for the New York Yankees from 1950 until 1967, an era that can easily be described as a second golden age for the Bronx ball club. Ford retired with an astounding 236-106 record. And before you jump up whining that pretty much *anybody* could have done well when backed by those legendary Yankee teams, I'll also point out that Ford retired with a 2.75 ERA, *still* the lowest for starters in the modern live-ball period.

I am absolutely sure regarding two of the kids who attended the game that night. One was a fellow named John O'Brien, a boy whose family lived about five houses down from mine. He was friendly but not really a friend, as he was several years younger than I. The other kid who was definitely there was…yours truly. There were probably three or four others as well, but they don't much figure into this nostalgic little tale.

I'm also not sure that John was even that big a baseball fan, but that didn't stop him from repeatedly bringing up the fact that his mother Peggy had gone to school with Whitey Ford. It seemed to be, at least for that particular evening, his one claim to fame. It was his personal brush with greatness, once removed, and it made him very proud indeed.

As luck would have it after the game we hung around the parking lot where the Yankees parked their cars and who should come strolling along but the legendary Whitey Ford himself. Ballplayers were happy to sign autographs in those days, and for free, so we all began pushing slips of paper through the eight-foot tall chain-link fence for Whitey to sign. Some kids even tossed baseballs over the fence, which the obliging pitcher caught, signed and tossed back.

John stood there shyly until, unable to keep it in any longer, he said, "Hey Whitey, my mother went to high school with you. Peggy O' Brien." And without missing a beat Whitey looked at him and answered, "Oh yeah, how is she?"

Well John's personal stock soared at that moment. He seemed to suddenly have been puffed up like a balloon in a Thanksgiving parade. He floated, and the rest of us walked, back to the car for the long ride from the threatening Bronx back to the safety of the Long Island suburbs.

We were about halfway home when my brain, never at rest for long, churned out a bit of information that I found so interesting I thought I'd share it with the group. And especially with John, who was still basking in the warming glow generated from his fame-induced contact high.

"You know John, back in high school your mother's name wasn't Peggy O'Brien. She wasn't married yet."

Well needless to say the poor kid's face dropped like a Bush approval rating, but what could I do? It was the truth and I felt he needed to know. Just call me the little old balloon popper.

Yes, Whitey Ford, legendary ace pitcher for the New York Yankees and future member of baseball's Hall of Fame, had lied to a little kid. Oh sure the lie was an act of kindness to spare the kid's feelings, but it was a lie none the less. I, on the other hand, had let nothing stand in the way of the truth, even if the truth mercilessly crushed the young and fragile spirit of an innocent kid. Why, it's not inconceivable that, due to my bold revelation, John could be in therapy to this very day.

Yeah, back in 1964 Whitey Ford was a much nicer person than I. Hell, he probably still is.

Tales of Unspeakable Woe: Good-bye, Santa

The class was clearly divided into two factions. I, showing early signs of the leadership skills that, sadly, would never develop past the embryonic stage, headed one of those factions. Michelle, my buck-toothed and not unhomely blonde classmate, led the other.

"I saw my parents putting the presents under the Christmas tree!" said Michelle with a passion approaching religious fervor. Or more accurately, "I thaw my parenth putting the presenth under the Chrithmath tree!" In addition to her many other shortcomings Michelle had a tendency to lisp when she spoke, each utterance unfailingly accompanied by an unwelcome shower of spit. Say it, don't spray it, my mother would have told her.

The debate had been raging for well over an hour now, and our second grade class was approaching near chaos and in danger of falling into complete anarchy. Still, the debate continued and I, for one, was not about to give up the fight. I couldn't believe that Michelle, along with her small army of dim-witted toadies, was still insisting that there was no such thing as Santa Claus. Evil thinking like that simply had to be stopped no matter what the cost, I thought, and I was just the chubby little seven-year old to do it!

Finally our teacher, the now-infamous Mrs. Quartucci, had apparently had enough and decided it was time to reestablish control over her over-heated brood. She told everyone to take their seats and then she began the speech that still haunts me over half a century later.

No, I don't remember it word-for-word. How could I, after the passing of so much time? But believe me, I remember the gist of what Mrs. Quartucci told our class of about thirty six and seven year old children. Boy, do I ever:

"We enjoy many holidays in our country. And most of those holidays have a symbol of some sort that we associate with it. For example, when we think of the Fourth of July we might think of the flag, or fireworks. On Halloween there are pumpkins, and who knows what a symbol for Thanksgiving might be? Right, a turkey. Yes, or a Pilgrim. Now when we think about Christmas we think about Santa Claus. So that's what Santa Claus is, children, he's just a symbol for the holiday of Christmas..."

I was stunned. In fact I was as stunned as I had ever been in my short life, and so I sat there and stared straight ahead, desperately trying to process what Mrs. Quartucci had just said. I resisted the urge to glance over at Michelle, who was without a doubt staring at me at that very moment, all smug and self-satisfied, with her spit-flecked chin jutted cruelly and victoriously in my direction.

Now after a quick analysis I realized that Mrs. Quartucci hadn't actually said that there was no such thing as Santa. And yet her meaning was almost unmistakable. Still, there was room for doubt about what I thought I'd heard, and so I sucked it up, struggled through the rest of the school day (avoiding any contact with that gargoyle

Michelle) and went home to discuss the issue and hopefully get a clarification from Mom.

I told Mom what Mrs. Quartucci had said, and then I cried, and then cried some more. Mom tried her best to console her devastated son, but she didn't have to say a word. I had already realized exactly what Mrs. Quartucci had told the class, and the look on Mom's face confirmed that my teacher had been speaking the truth. There was no such thing as Santa Claus.

Well into my fifties Mom would tell me that she should have called the school to complain on that day. But at the time she was a young mother with three children to raise, and it was the 1950's. Polite young women did not make trouble or in any way undermine a teacher's authority. Today, of course, Mrs. Quartucci would most likely been slapped with a lawsuit before the sun had set, and would have probably ended up enjoying a successful career serving burgers and fries to the families of the children she used to teach.

There are millions of people in this country who believe that a topic such as sexual education should not be taught in our schools. This is something that should be taught in the home, they proclaim, sometimes quite loudly. And while this may or may not be true, a part of me can understand their point of view. I feel the same way about Santa Claus. And now, at this late date, there is little that can be done to repair the damage done to that little boy by people like Mrs. Quartucci. But there may be something. I figure it like this: my best guess is that Mrs.

Quartucci was nearly sixty years old when she dropped her bombshell on the class. And so by combining that fact with the knowledge that this event happened fifty-one years ago we can do a little math, add the numbers, carry the six and, ipso fatso, there you have it.

You see, numbers never lie. And so next Christmas what I think I'm going to do is march myself down to the mall, hop onto the lap of the nearest Santa Claus and tell him and all that with listen that today, here in the 21st century, there is without a doubt no such thing as Mrs. Quartucci.

Bless Me Father

I don't know of any stronger evidence to prove what a good little Catholic boy I was than the fact that my very first date involved taking a girl to confession. Confession, for those of you who were not lucky enough to be raised in the wild, wacky world of Catholicism, is that ritual where you kneel in a dark closet and confess your sins through a screen to a priest who is sitting in his own dark closet. The priest has a confessor on either side of him and slides a panel shut when he is done with you and ready to turn his attention to the sinner on the other side. It's an efficient process and it keeps those long Saturday afternoon lines moving. In fact, it's a system that is still ahead of its time, and should have been picked up by the Burger King drive-through years ago.

Now why we were required to tell our crimes to a priest and have him pass them along to God remains somewhat of a mystery. Who was this guy, God's receptionist? Also, at times when you were awaiting your turn to spill your guts you could hear the person confessing on the other side. It was your job not to listen, no matter how much of an abomination the confessed crimes might be. And I never did listen. Nope, not even once. Not as far as you know.

As a kid my brother often claimed that once when he entered the confessional (creative name for that closet, eh?) he saw the priest was reading an Archie comic. Back then I never believed this story but, as my brother continued to swear to its veracity well into adulthood, I believe it now. I believe it for two reasons: first, if my brother was going to make up a story why not take the dramatics all the way to the edge and claim that the priest was reading a Playboy or nudie rag? And second, if I was a priest that's probably what I would do. What could be more relaxing and peaceful on a hot summer day than sitting in a dark, quiet booth in air-conditioned comfort and enjoying the latest adventures of Archie and Jughead? Nothing, that's what.

The hard part, of course, was the actual confessing of your sins. Not just admitting to them, but remembering them. Although believe me, the offenses you admitted to went through the heaviest of editing processes. For example, you could tell the priest that you had fought with your brother three times in the past month, and that might be fairly accurate. Especially if you failed to mention that each fight lasted about a week. But inevitably you'd get to the big ones, those chart-topping hit songs that everybody came to hear. And these were called, of course, "impure thoughts."

Now, how many times a month would you think a healthy pubescent young man, bursting with buckets of delicious hormones, would have an impure thought? Guys, of course, know the answer to this. Women, you don't want to know. Generally it seemed acceptable to tell the priest that I had had six to eight impure thoughts that month. In truth, I often had at least that many during the short time I kneeled in the dark waiting for the priest to slide that little panel open. But how could I give the guy an accurate number? It was just too embarrassing, not to mention impossible to compute. We didn't have calculators back then and I never did figure out how to work a slide rule.

Generally you were expected to go to confession about once a month. After that you were really taking a chance. As the weeks went by you felt dirtier and dirtier as your soul grew darker with the accumulating stains of your filthy sins. It was risky business, because if you happened to, say, be squashed by a speeding cement truck while wallowing in this impure state, well sonny, you just bought yourself a direct ticket--do not pass Go--to Hell. It was, in no small way, similar to getting caught in an accident while you were wearing dirty underwear.

You can laugh all you want at the concept of confession (And I do. Frequently.) but from a psychological point of view you can see the value. What else gives you a fresh start, each and every month, no matter what vile things you've done? It was like the psychotherapy of its day, except it was free! Sure, there were those who quipped that they could commit any evil deed they chose, because they'd just have it forgiven in confession in a week or so. These delusional saps thought they had found a spiritual loophole, but of course they hadn't. (See previous paragraph re: cement truck.)

And so at the age of thirteen I began my first official date by walking to Janie's house and then the two of us walked through the bare trees and chilly air to the church about a mile away. We both made our confession and then knelt at the altar to do our assigned penance, usually a few prayers. Janie got up first and began to walk down the aisle of the church towards the exit, and I immediately followed.

As I walked behind her, my hands clasped reverently as if still in prayer, I thought about how wonderful it felt to again be washed free of sin. And how lucky I was to be here on this special and holy day with Janie, who I'd had a crush on since fourth grade. And how great she looked, especially from this angle, with her firm young buttocks subtly twitching with each step beneath the thin fabric of the tight flowered pants that--damn! I had already soiled my newly purified soul and I hadn't even gotten it out of the church!

You Rot

It's funny how some expressions die out, while others get passed down from generation to generation. For example, when is the last time you heard something described using 1920's jargon such as the "bee's knees" or the "cat's pajamas"? Aside from in these essays, I mean.

We had, of course, our own slang terms growing up in the '60's. Groovy, far out and right on were all common phrases forty or so years ago. And yet you rarely hear them now. Oh okay, I'll admit to still using "groovy" once in a while, but that's only to amuse the young ones. They seem to get such a kick out of it.

One expression that seems to glide effortlessly through each era is "cool." When I was a kid anything, or anyone, that had gained your approval was cool. Before my time (yes, there really was such a thing) DA haircuts, cigarette packs rolled up into shirt sleeves and Elvis were all cool. Today there's even a star named LL Cool J, although who he might be or what he might do I have no idea. And through all these generations that burning desire remains the same: everybody wants to be cool. Hell, even at this late date I still cling to the hope that I might yet achieve cool status, although to be honest the hopes are diminishing with my eyesight.

And yet there is one slang term that I recall but nobody else seems to. I suspect, but can't say for sure, that its use was geographically limited to the East Coast. And even if it was, when I talk today to my contemporaries of the time--friends, relatives, strangers--nobody remembers using the term themselves, or even hearing it, no matter where they grew up. Yet I'm telling you that as kids, for whatever brief period of time, the word was constantly on our lips. We used it daily, many times a day, to describe all manner of things.

The word was "rot." It was used as the exact opposite of cool. When you disapproved of something, be it a TV show, song, or even a directive from your parents, a proper response was "this rots." And it could be applied to people too, and it was. Frequently, to friends and foes alike. If your buddy cut you off on his bicycle or your brother took the last Ho-Ho, each could expect to hear a loud and definitive "You rot!" in his near future. And he wouldn't get particularly offended either, because while we recognized that "you rot!" was really a form of "fuck you!" it was milder and more benign. Why, when used correctly "you rot" could be perceived as downright friendly!

I don't know when "rot" went out of style, but I do know what replaced it. Today it's common to hear kids say that something, or someone, "sucks." It's still surprises me that the expression has caught on like it has, because those of us who remember its rise also recall that it once was, like "jerk" and "dope" in an earlier time, a rather shocking and even obscene term, certainly not appropriate for public expression. Of course it wasn't the two-word term "you suck" that was so blatantly offensive, but the original three, four or even five word phrase that caused alarm. And remember, it wasn't the fact that you sucked, but more exactly *what* you sucked, that created such consternation. And I'll leave the rest to your imagination.

Thinking about it I was surprised to realize that "you suck" goes back further than even I realized. In fact, I was suddenly able to recall an incident that occurred on the school bus when I was in high school. It involved a cranky old bus driver and a student named Billy T., a hapless, although by no means innocent, young fellow whose unfortunate use of the expression "you suck" led to dire consequences that I've no doubt he still speaks of today. Probably to his shrink.

You Suck

Above I mentioned that it was possible, at times, to use the terms "you rot" or "you suck" in a friendly, joking sort of way. This wasn't one of those times. And, thank God, it wasn't me who said it. But I was on that school bus.

And so was Billy T. It was the end of the school day and a nearly-full bus was pulling away from our high school. Suddenly some of the students began to shout at the driver. "Stop!" "Wait!" "Somebody else is coming!" Despite the ardent and somewhat loud pleas, the driver continued to pull away from the school and proceeded on his regular route. The tardy student, whoever he might have been, had now missed the bus, and there was much grumbling amongst my fellow passengers.

At this point you'll be agreeing with the angry students. Why couldn't the driver simply have stopped, opened his door and let the poor fellow on? Why, indeed? And while I can't justify the driver's actions of that day forty years ago, I believe that time has given me a bit of perspective, a glimpse into what might have been going through that driver's head when he so arrogantly pulled away from the curb.

His name was Morris and we looked upon him as a cranky, grizzled old man. He was probably about forty. I don't know how long he had been a school bus driver or how long he continued in that career after this incident. Not long, I suspect.

We had had many drivers over the years and each dealt with their situation in their own way. The situation, of course, was how to keep your cool while navigating a twelve-ton school bus in heavy traffic while behind your back forty or so young punks were plotting God knows what. One young driver befriended many of the students, going so far as to swap cigarettes with some of the "cooler" girls. An older woman driver smiled and joked constantly, all the while her eyes revealing the "please don't kill me" thoughts that were racing inside her skull. And then there was Morris.

I think that Morris, too, was frightened. I don't think he wanted to be driving that bus (Who would?) nor did he trust a single one of those rowdy, cocksure teens lurking in the rows behind him. He was simply afraid, and when those hooligans began to shout for him to stop he ignored them, probably not knowing why they were yelling or caring much if he did. Whatever trickery they were up to, he wanted no part of it. The sooner he began his run the sooner his bus would return to the empty and peaceful state he much preferred.

Not everyone on that bus was content to just grumble at Morris for his blatantly inconsiderate act. Remember, this is the story of Billy T., and it was he who would shout out at the bus driver, and would be clearly heard; by Morris and by everybody else on that bus. Yes, Billy T. yelled out but two words on that day. The words were, "You suck!"

Suddenly for Morris, making a left turn and returning to the school's front drive was within the realm of the possible. You could tell he was having an "I don't have to take this shit" moment. Heck, he might have even been taught this by his instructor in school bus driving school.

"You don't have to take any shit from those kids, Morris," the instructor may have said,

And so we sat in the re-parked bus in front of the school, and waited and waited. And then he arrived: the assistant principal. The discipline guy. The hard-ass. The man who never smiled. He spoke quietly with Morris and then began to slowly walk down that narrow school bus aisle, glaring at each of us as he did.

"Who said it?" he snarled.

Nobody confessed or, to our credit, squealed.

"This bus isn't going anywhere until I know who said it."

You know the scene. It's been featured in any number of prisoner of war movies. And as in those movies, the tension was almost unbearable. And then Billy did the noble thing and spoke up. Well, the semi-noble thing, anyway.

"Uh, all I said was 'my socks' because my friend was supposed to bring..."

"Let's go," said the Assistant principal, not buying Billy's story for a millisecond.

Laugh if you must at Billy's vain "sock" attempt to free himself, but for me I give him credit. In that short period of time, under that kind of pressure, I think he did the best he could. I would even go so far to say that his faux excuse was downright creative, and might well have worked on a different teacher on a different day. But not on this day, and certainly not on this teacher.

Billy and the assistant principal disappeared into the dark interior of the nearly empty school, the bus door closed and we were again, more silent now, on our way. No, I do not know if the late student whose tardiness had triggered the incident took this opportunity to board the bus. If so, I hope someone made him aware that Billy T. had died for his sins.

Later that day I was riding my bicycle when a car drove by. I casually looked in the window and saw that Billy T. was sitting in the passenger seat. He wasn't a close friend, but I knew him and instinctively I lifted my arm to wave. And then I realized what was going on.

The none-too-happy-looking driver of the car was obviously Billy's father, and they were just returning from what must have been a torturous meeting with the assistant principal, followed by an equally tortuous and interminable ride back home. I dropped my hand as Billy, blank faced, continued to stare straight ahead. He never knew I was there. Now, I don't know what actually happened to Billy T. once he and his father got home and the front door was shut behind them, but I suspect it really sucked.

What I Should Have Said: The Year Jesus Was Born

I was nine years old and spending another of my precious and dwindling childhood Saturday mornings at what the adults called "Religious Instruction" but was more commonly known among us kids as Catechism. To the adults' credit, the very idea of creating a religious training class that would be held on Saturdays was as brilliant as it was devious.

"Let's see," they surely must have mused. "The little bastards are trapped in a schoolroom from Monday through Friday and then we force them to church on Sunday. But what about Saturday? Surely we can't have them walking around all free and happy for an entire day. What to do, what to do..."

What, indeed. And so Catechism was born and we were sent to spend an hour and a half of every Saturday wedged into those uncomfortable wood and metal Catholic school desks that were surely antique torture devices left over from the good old days of the Inquisition. What could possibly have made this situation any worse?

"And let's have the classes taught by nuns."

And so it was. I recall one particular Saturday we were given an exercise to complete, an exercise that, had it not been for the itchy clothes, uncomfortable chair and evil-looking woman dressed as a penguin who constantly glared down at us, might have actually been fun. Well, if not fun, tolerable.

We were asked to list the numbers from one to ten on a sheet of paper, and next to each we were to give an example of how that number would apply to something in the Catholic religion. For example, next to the number one I might write, "There is one God." Easy. Next to two I put, "Jesus had two natures." (The nature of Man and the nature of God, for you heathens. You're going to Hell, you know.)

I was chugging through my list quite nicely when I came to number five. Now I couldn't even imagine what my dull and predictable classmates had come up with for that number. Jesus had five toes on his right foot? But the mundane and ordinary was not for *this* budding religious scholar. Yep, here I go again.

I had recently read an article that mentioned that historians had shown that Jesus had probably been born prior to 4 BC, and most likely in the year 5 BC. The article went on and on explaining how those godless eggheads had arrived at this date, but really all I needed for Catechism class was the number. And so after number five I wrote, "Jesus was born in 5 BC." And listen, before you anticipate what's coming and get to feeling too sorry for me, trust me, I knew what I was doing. I knew that I was busting balls.

"This is ridiculous," sniffed the black-habited nun as she looked down at my paper. "Everybody knows that Jesus was born in the year zero." And then she dismissed me with a heavy sigh of disgust and whooshed past my desk, on her way to berate the next student.

And so I hung my head, remained silent and tried to content myself with the knowledge that I knew something that the nun did not. It was a hollow, empty feeling.

WHAT I *SHOULD* HAVE SAID:

You ignorant bitch! Did they teach you one damn thing in nun school besides self-righteous indignation and keeping your knees together? Let me take you through this s-l-o-w-l-y and maybe, just maybe, you'll learn something today. First of all, who was king when Jesus was born? C'mon, I know you know this one. Right, Herod the Great. And in what year did Herod die? No, I didn't think you did. Well, it was in 4 BC. Right after, according to legend, that's right I said legend, he ordered the death of every male child in Bethlehem under the age of two. Listen, am I getting through here? So tell me, if that weird starched nun-hat of yours isn't constricting the blood flow to your already feeble brain, how did Herod order the death of a child over four years after he himself died? Fuck this place--I'll come back when Jesus returns.

What I Should Have Said: Last Night at Dinner

I'm sitting in my third-grade class and my regular teacher Miss Davvy is not there. Why? Who knows? Flu, hangover, torrid affair with a married man? At eight years old you don' think about such things; you couldn't even begin to imagine the vile goings-on that were taking place at the adult level. I often wish it had stayed that way.

Standing in front of us was our substitute teacher. Her name and her appearance has been long lost to the foggy recesses, and that's just fine with me. What hasn't been lost is the writing assignment she had given us. Two hours earlier I had distinctly heard her tell the class to write a story, and the title of this story should be "Last Night at Dinner."

Instantly my brain flashed like a Central Park pervert. Let the rest of these third-grade slobs write about the fried pork chops and mashed potatoes their bone-weary mother had served to the family while their alcoholic father burped and slobbered behind the daily newspaper. That's fine for this collection of uninspired knuckleheads I called classmates, but not for a literary wunderkind like me!

And so I proceeded to write a delightfully imaginative tale set in the days of old. In it a king had been losing all of his best men as he sent each to slay the terrible dragon that was destroying the village. And now, as he sat consuming his evening meal, he looked across the table at the only man who remained alive who had any chance of finally slaying the horrid creature. Yes, the king had to place all of his hope in this, the "Last Knight at Dinner." Get it? Get it?

Well she didn't. The substitute teacher stood in front of the class and read what even now I can only describe as my work of unadulterated genius, and then she said these never-to-be-forgotten words:

"Well, this is a nice story, but it has nothing to do with the assignment. I distinctly said to write a story called, "At Dinner Last Night."

I responded by hanging my head and consoling myself with the fact that at least she had said it was a nice story.

WHAT I SHOULD HAVE SAID:

You ignorant bitch! You did not say "At Dinner Last Night," you said "Last Night at Dinner." If you can't even keep the assignment straight that you yourself made up, how do you expect us to? And even if you did change the wording a bit, a simple, focused reading of the four-word title should have allowed even an obvious dope like yourself to recognize the pun. I don't know if you're drunk or just stupid, but it's a shock to me that they'd even let you in here to scrub the floors, much less teach. Take the twenty bucks you're earning today and go buy yourself a clue. Fuck this place--I'll be back tomorrow when Miss Davvy returns.

What I Should Have Said: Gold Stars in My Catechism

It's a year later and I'm suffering through another Saturday Catechism class; new nun, same old dogma. And although this nun is big on memorization, she also seems to have some vague sense of the value of positive reinforcement. At the beginning of each year every student is given a Catechism. (Actually I have no doubt that we were required to pay for them, but I don't recall the specifics right now.)

You know what a Catechism actually is, don't you? It's a paperback book containing every conceivable question about the Catholic religion that a little soon-to-be-brainwashed boy or girl could ask. Well, not *every* question. For example, once a classmate asked the nun if it was a sin to kill if you were in a war. The nun sputtered a bit, regained some traction and said that she would have the priest come in to answer that one. He never showed.

But all the basics were there. "Who made you? God made me. Who is God? God is our heavenly father who made Heaven and Earth and all things, blah, blah, blah." Well, if it's *not* brainwashing how come I still remember this nonsense after half a century?

What the nun wanted us to do was to memorize the answer (word for word!) to each question in the book, a chapter at a time. When we were ready she would come to our desk and ask us each question, and if we got the entire chapter correct we'd get a reward. Now as far as I'm concerned here's where our nun fell short. I can't speak for my other classmates but I myself would have thought that something like a candy bar or a comic book would be a terrific reward for a twelve year old boy. (Or perhaps some Girl Scout cookies, or even a Girl Scout.)

But no, what you got from the nun for perfecting a chapter of questions was...a gold star. Yes, one of those shiny things that you lick and stick right on the Catechism page. (Now I'm desperately trying to remember: Did she actually *lick* all of my gold stars? Was my cherished Catechism actually held together by little more than gobs of nun slobber? Ew!)

Despite my ceaseless whining here, I actually welcomed the task of memorizing the Catechism. No, I wasn't all het up by the fires of a deep religious fervor. I just liked the challenge and welcomed the competition. And so I began at the beginning: "Who made you? God made me..."

Listen, I ripped through those chapters like Oprah tearing through a buffet. One gold star, three, seven. I was unstoppable. How was I doing compared to the rest of my less-inspired classmates? I had no way of knowing. That is, until that day.

We were about halfway through the year when the nun told us to settle down, because she had something to say. She wanted to know how many gold stars each of us had earned. Finally! Here I was, the Gold Star Boy and now was my chance to shine!

She started off with the sad little underachievers.

"How many of you have one gold star?" asked the nun as I stifled a guffaw. Two or three losers raised their loser hands.

"Two? Three? Four?"

With each number called a small number of kids raised their hands. Right up until the nun got up to number nine, when nobody raised their hands. When the nun asked "Ten?" and no hands were raised she began to address the class.

"Now you people are just going to have to study a lot harder. You need to read your Catechism and learn all those questions, because if you don't you'll find out that--"

Huh? That was it? The nun was done calling out numbers? Here I was nearly peeing my pants with giddy anticipation, waiting to hear my number called. My number, incidentally, was fourteen. Yes, I had in my now-worn Catechism fourteen gold stars soaked in nun spit, and now the world would never know of my monumental achievement. I sat there stunned, hung my head and quietly gave myself a mental pat on the back. It was quite an accomplishment, really, no matter who knew.

WHAT I SHOULD HAVE SAID:

You ignorant bitch! Why did you stop calling numbers? Didn't they teach you to count that high in nun school? Listen, I don't expect you to know the exact amount of gold stars you gave to each student, but Jesus Christ in a green hat, you came to my desk fourteen times and I gave you fourteen perfect performances. How could you not remember that? It seems you don't even have the awareness that God gave a doorknob. Fuck this place. I'll come back when you wake up and start giving out candy bars. Or Girl Scouts.

Uncle Joe Fish

I met a guy tonight whose last name is Fish, and this reminded me of my own Uncle Joe Fish. Now Uncle Joe Fish was not technically my uncle, but my great-uncle, and his last name was not Fish. As far as I know, however, his first name was indeed Joe.

Uncle Joe's last name was Italian, my mother's maiden name, and its first syllable is pronounced "vish," so it's not hard to figure the derivation of the nickname. The truth is I never knew that Uncle Joe was called Joe Fish until long after the last time I saw him. My brothers and I didn't see Uncle Joe very often, and at this late date I'm a little sad to think that, aside from a face in the crowd at the all-too-common funerals, I have only one distinct memory of Uncle Joe. Ah, but it's a good one.

My two brothers and I was spending a week at my grandparents--the German side--in Ozone Park, New York, giving my parents their annual, and probably much appreciated, respite from, well, my two brothers and I. Uncle Joe, also being from Ozone Park, dropped by for a visit. What I recall is Uncle Joe sitting on the cement steps of my grandparents' house, opening his wallet, and attempting to hand a dollar bill to each of us. We, of course, refused.

My brothers and I had been aggressively conditioned, and to this day I'm not exactly sure why, to refuse anything that might be offered to us. It now seems to me that it was politeness training gone horribly awry. If someone offered us a cookie we would politely respond, "No, thank you." This was no matter how desperately we wanted that cookie, which I have no doubt we always did. We might be offered a cold soda on a sweltering day, and again our response would still be, "No, thank you." Hell, we could have been standing there being consumed by flames and if offered a bucket of water it's an even bet that our response would have been, "No, thank you."

Well, Uncle Joe was having none of it. After our third or fourth refusal Uncle Joe simply took the three bills and threw them into the air, smiling broadly with a "Now what are you going to do?" expression on his face. Well, we knew *exactly* what we were going to do. With this unexpected and outrageous act all the rules of politeness were off. Remember, this was a time when going to the movies cost a quarter and a candy bar was a nickel. Uncle Joe had just flung the modern equivalent of over twenty bucks into the air and we thought him delightfully mad. It wasn't very long before we were each clutching a dollar and eagerly thanking our mother's seemingly crazed uncle.

Just a few months ago I mentioned Uncle Joe to Dad, who said that he'd been "connected." I'd heard this before, of course, but how connected Joe actually was is really anybody's guess. Those who knew for sure have all passed on. Maybe they died from natural causes or maybe some of them are "sleeping with the fishes." It's unlikely that Uncle Joe was anything more than a numbers-runner for the mob, if that, but who knows? Is it possible that this same man who laughed as he watched us kids chase after those dollar bills could have once pushed some cement-shoed squealer off a boat, launching him on a non-stop, one-way trip to the bottom of Jamaica Bay? Well, if he did this, the victim, like my brothers and I, must have also thought that Joe Fish was crazed and outrageous. Although perhaps not delightfully so.

Uncle Vito

If you had said to me just yesterday, "Quick, was Uncle Vito a blood relation to you?" I would have probably have fumfered around trying to figure out the answer. The answer, I'm a little surprised to learn, was no. Uncle Vito, another of my mother's uncles, was married to Aunt Rosie, my mother's mother's sister. Uncle Vito was, however, the first dead person I ever knew.

Like with Uncle Joe, I have but one fond memory of Uncle Vito, and that was the time he came to stay with us for a few days. The reason? He was going to help my dad put in a patio at our house. Whether Uncle Vito had a background in this sort of thing I don't know. That information is lost to the ages. Maybe he had provided the cement that Uncle Joe Fish used to, well, you know. I *do* remember perceiving Uncle Vito as a rather old, and rather colorful, man. What his age might have been, who knows? It's very possible that he was actually younger then than I am right now. Hell, I was only about ten and my parents were still in their thirties. Uncle Vito might have been 45 and seemed to me a fossil.

It turned out that Uncle Vito was an early riser, and not a quiet one. Each morning he would rouse the household by singing, "You gotta get up, you gotta get up, you gotta get up in the m-o-o-o-o-r-ning!" This was bellowed out, of course, to the tune of "Reveille." Clearly at some point Uncle Vito had been in the army and like many others who had also served in the military, at least to my sleep-deprived ten year old mind, he didn't seem to quite know when to let it go.

Once we had all been jolted awake it was time for Uncle Vito to have his "coffee." And that's how we all said it too, "coffee" in quotation marks. Now the exact proportions might have faded from my memory over the last half century, but it's a good guess that Uncle Vito's quote coffee consisted of about one part honest-to-god coffee to three parts whiskey. You gotta get up in the morning!

The patio, when completed, would remain a family joke right up until, and for some time after, it was redone two or three years later, this time by professionals. Sober professionals. The standard line when one walked across Uncle Vito's wavy cement creation was, "I'm getting seasick!" Whether Uncle Vito was paid for his "expertise," had done it as a favor or simply had shown up for the free hooch I couldn't say. I was not privy to such information. I was ten.

Years later it was our turn to visit Uncle Vito, and my two brothers and I, accompanied by Dad, entered the darkened bedroom where Uncle Vito lay dying of cancer. At home Mom had suggested to my youngest brother that it might cheer up Uncle Vito if he sang a little of "You Gotta Get Up" to him. When the time came my brother, although prompted by my father, refused to sing the song. And who could blame him? Uncle Vito, however, flat on his back and semi-conscious, had caught the gist of the conversation and answered, "No, I don't think I'll be getting up in the morning." And he never did.

Thirty-One

I miss playing Thirty-One. It's a simple yet surprisingly fun card game I used to play in Florida, usually with my brother, mother and Spike. (Dad, at the first sign of a deck of cards, instantly retreated to the bedroom to watch that week's football or baseball Game of the Century.)

I won't go into every detail and rule of the game. These, I'm sure, can be found online. Quickly though, each player is dealt three cards and the goal is to get a total of, yup, thirty-one. Play begins with three dimes in front of each player. After the conclusion of each hand-- after one player has "knocked"--the player with the lowest score has to toss a dime into the pot. Once a player has lost all of his or her dimes he is then "on his honor." One more loss and he's out of the game.

Questions arise. Can the game be played with other than dimes? Say with nickels, quarters, paper clips or Krugerrands? Certainly, but not at our house. We could have had a garbage pail full of nickels and we'd still be scrounging around the house looking for dimes. Because Thirty-One is always played with dimes. Also, what's the point of "on your honor?" Wouldn't it be the same to just start with *four* dimes? Yes, but again, not at our house.

It seemed that more often than not, as we approached the end of the game, the number of wins each person had was about the same. Nobody would know this, of course, if old anal-retentive Leonard wasn't methodically keeping score. For example, my mom, brother and I might have two wins each, with my wife Spike with one. My brother, whining for at least a half-hour that he "had to go home," would graciously agree to play one more hand. This was my cue to point out what I thought should be fairly obvious to everyone:

"Okay, one more hand," I'd agree. "That is, unless Spike wins. Then, of course, we'd all have two wins and would necessarily play one more hand to declare the night's winner."

"I'm only playing one more hand," grumped my brother.

"Yes. Unless Spike wins. Then we have to play one more," I'd explain patiently.

"I don't care who wins, I'm going home. I have to get to bed!"

"It's 9:30. What are you, a farmer? You have to get up early to milk the cows?"

And so we'd play. And sometimes Spike, or whoever it was on that particular night, would get that win and we'd be all tied up. And would my brother stay to play that all-important tie-breaker? Sometimes, if I browbeat him enough, he would. And then we'd have an overall winner, a champion for that evening. Just as we should. And sometimes he'd just get up and leave.

Was part of the fun for me the laughing and teasing of my brother, and using every trick in the book to get him to stay for that final game? Of course. But then again, there's still the part of me than can' t even begin to comprehend how you can have a four-way tie and not have a championship game, an ultimate winner. What would be the point of playing?

The Ten Dollar Skis

I don't remember what had happened to my previous pair of skis, if indeed I had actually owned a previous pair. Nor do I remember how I ended up the owner of a set of fairly-new bindings with no skis attached. This happened, after all, over four decades ago. I only know that my childhood chum Lenny and I were scheduled to go skiing that weekend and I now found myself not one but *two* skis short of the optimal number. I could always have rented a pair, but that process would take away much valuable time on the slopes. And so Lenny and I headed to Morsan's, a Long Island sporting goods store that may or may not still be in business.

Wait, check that! I remember now. We went to Morsan's to see about renting skis, but then while there I discovered *them*. A pair of shiny new skis that cost only ten dollars. Sure they weren't a name brand, and they may well have been the last pair of skis on the East Coast made out of wood, but they cost ten dollars. I could own a pair of skis for less than the price of renting them. Hell, even if I only got one winter out of them they'd be an incredible bargain. To me, the choice seemed obvious.

Back home I mentioned to Lenny that we'd have to go back to Morsan's to get the bindings put on. I can't be definite about his reaction--this was forty years ago-- but I'm pretty sure he scoffed. "We can put them on the skis ourselves," he said, a concept that was about as alien to me as time travel. But my friend insisted, grabbed my dad's drill and before I knew it we, and by that I mean "he", had attached the bindings in what appeared to be a professional manner.

There was a great deal that I enjoyed about skiing. I loved the crisp fresh air, the snowy mountain scenery, the patches from places I'd skied sewn onto my jacket sleeve, the après ski hot chocolate and the lift ticket I kept in my coat's zipper tab for months, just to impress the chicks. The skiing itself had its moments, of course, but frankly I could take it or leave it. Our first run of the day went just fine. The sun was out, the snow was powder and I hadn't run into any trees. The second run of the day was pretty much the same.

It was on my third run, about halfway down, that I took a hard fall into the fluffy snow. When I heard the snap I waited for a second or two, until I was reassured that the sharp sound that had travelled unobstructed through the frigid air had not come from inside my priceless body but rather from one of my much less valuable wooden skis. A quick glance, and the lack of excruciating pain, confirmed that one of my new skis had broken cleanly in two.

Lenny couldn't believe it when I declared I was done for the day. There was lots of daytime left, and to him the only sensible thing to do would be for me to now rent a pair of (hopefully higher quality) skis and head back up the hill. My definition of sensible varied somewhat, and included heading for the lodge, buying a new patch for my sleeve and regaling an assortment of snow bunnies with the dramatic tale of my harrowing, ski-breaking run as I warmed myself with a hot chocolate in front of the blazing fire. And that's just what I did.

The next weekend found me back at Morsan's, complaining about the performance of the ten dollar skis they had sold me. Full of righteous indignation, I boldly demanded a refund, a refund that was readily given in the form of a store credit. I walked around the sporting goods store and with my new-found wealth clutched in my hand, eventually settled on a khaki knapsack that would last me throughout my college career and for many years to come.

In fact, if I dig around the dusty boxes in my garage it may well still be crammed in there somewhere. Unlike those cheap-ass skis, which were rewarded for their granting me an early reprieve from the slopes with an ignoble burial in a Dumpster at the back of a rustic, snow-covered lodge. The bindings, it should be said, remained securely attached.

The Sump

It was called a sump. I didn't know why then, and today, over forty years later, I still don't. You would think that having in huge hole in the ground right on the other side of your backyard would be a wondrous asset to the boys and girls in the neighbor, and I suppose growing up we might have thought it was. And yet even then I'm sure that I wasn't the only one with the nagging feeling that in reality the sump was somehow falling far short of our youthful expectations. Some would say that was good training for the life ahead.

Now, this sump wasn't just some ditch or minor depression in the ground. It was large enough that it might remind you of a small quarry, and was so long we couldn't have thrown a stone from one side to the other. Not lengthwise, anyway. You got to the muddy bottom of it by walking down an earthen ramp, no doubt designed for heavy-equipment vehicles that never returned. At the bottom you'd discover its most interesting feature, a cement tunnel with a crosshatching of iron bars to keep out curious young knuckleheads much like ourselves. The tunnel was clearly for the transport of water, although whether in *to* or out *of* the sump we couldn't say. We'd never seen that tunnel do much of anything.

There was a six-foot fence completely circling the sump, every inch of it topped with a healthy dose of barbed wire. There was a gate, also topped with barbed wire and perpetually locked. So what? We rarely saw anybody official unlock that gate, and once we had hopped the fence, usually at the cost of a tear or two of our thick denim jeans or our fair white skin, we never saw anybody inside. Which is not to say that playing in the sump did not come with that delicious combination of fear and rebellion, which we so valued in youth.

Ah, but there was the problem. Once over the fence and inside the sump there was nothing to *do* there. The idea of going to the sump, it turned out, was much more exciting than actually being there. Once or twice we brought our baseball mitts and tried to play ball, but the flat bottom of the sump really didn't include a wide enough area and, as previously mentioned, it was usually muddy besides. We could climb the slopes a bit and try throwing the ball around from there, but this was awkward and disorienting, like being caught in an M.C. Escher picture.

In winter we thought that the sides of the sump might be a wonderful place to go sledding, but here too the sump fell short of expectations. The sides were much too steep, and the ride ended on the bottom much too abruptly. And yes, it could, and would, often be muddy even in the winter.

There actually was another sump a mile or so away that did have some value to us kids. Unlike the one in my backyard this sump sometimes filled with water, water that froze in the winter. I can still remember when my brother and I took our ice skates and had a fine day gliding along the ice. Well, *I* had a fine day. My brother got a little too close to some thin ice and fell right on through, bounding out instantly, drenched and screaming all the way home as I followed behind carrying his skates. I'd like to think I wasn't laughing.

One year a new and wonderfully dangerous invention arrived. It was yellow and black and had a rope in the front to hold on to. I forget what they were called back then, but they were the great-great granddaddies of today's snowboards. They were cheap and made of wood, and it seemed that the ramp that descended to the bottom of the sump would be perfect for slides on these new-fangled toys. And once again, we were wrong. The ramp was pitted and gullied, and with a lunar scape of dirt clods and rocks that no amount of snow could cover up. Almost immediately the new boards were packed up with the sleds and brought to the groomed and gently sloping hills of the state park a few miles away.

And so eventually, if not consciously, the kids in the neighborhood found ourselves visiting the sump less and less, as if it were a childhood toy we'd outgrown. Then, as all kids do, we grew up, found exciting new interests, and rarely thought about the sump at all, if ever. And as I look back I can think of only one good thing that came out of the sump, and that was simply a clever line.

I had been telling a college girlfriend about the giant hole in my yard, and she admitted that she had never heard of such a thing. And so when the day came that she came for a visit of *course* the sump, along with the Empire State Building and The Statue of Liberty, was on her must-see list. We were twenty by this time and much too dignified to be climbing barb-wire fences. As it turned out we didn't need to. The gate was now unlocked, and apparently had been for a number of years. And why not? Neither the kids nor the county much cared about the sump anymore.

And so I took my girlfriend through the gate and we stood at the edge of the big hole. I may have made a grand sweeping gesture with my hand, as if I was showing off the Grand Canyon, although I'd like to think I didn't. And then, after a few minutes, we turned and walked back to the house. Well, I said to her, you have now, finally, seen the sump with your very own eyes. What do you think?

"That was sump-thing," she said.

The Spanky Club

I've already told you about the fantastic concerts they had at my college in the olden days. Many of these concerts were free, although some could cost as much as, well, two dollars. The artists who performed included such future legends as Fleetwood Mac, Yes, Graham Nash and Alice Cooper.

In addition to these concerts, however, the school also presented a lecture series, featuring some of the giants of the day in the fields of writing, art, history and political activism. Sadly, for whatever reason, I never availed myself of the opportunity to attend any of these speeches, as intellectually stimulating as I'm sure they must have been. I probably couldn't find the time to go because I was most likely off somewhere, you know, studying. Ahem.

Let me correct that. Among the Nobel nominees and poet laureates that I so easily skipped seeing, there was one speaker who I made a point not to miss. His name was George Robert Phillips McFarland. You might know him better as Spanky.

Now, it was the mid-seventies and Spanky was already 45 years old by the time he spoke to that lecture hall full of pseudo-hippies. He mostly talked about his years as the lead rascal in the classic *Our Gang* comedies of the 1930's. He showed a short clip from his original screen test for Hal Roach Studios, which was filmed shortly after his second birthday. And then he answered questions from the audience.

The marijuana-infused crowd was, for the most part, appreciative and respectful. Too young to have seen the original *Our Gang* shorts in movie theaters, we were however the first generation raised on television, and as such we knew Spanky well from watching the syndicated version of the classic films when they were repackaged for television as *The Little Rascals*.

But we were also, for the most part, well-educated, middle class white kids who, at the time, were convinced that we knew just about everything there was to know. (Life would later teach us otherwise.) And so we couldn't help but look down our noses just a bit at this fat old man (We were told, after all, not to trust anyone over 30.) with the poor grammar skills. And when at the end of the speech Spanky announced that we could each become a member of The Spanky Club by purchasing an official Spanky Club card on our way out, well you could almost hear the communal scoff of indignation.

Hey what kind of rip-off is this, man? I mean, we marched against Vietnam and for civil rights, have just about given Nixon the boot and we know crass commercialism when we see it. Sure, we might spend twenty bucks for a baggie of some brown and desiccated "Columbian," but a Spanky Club card? Just what are you trying to pull here?

After his run in *Our Gang*, Spanky found that he was horribly typecast, and he would have trouble finding acting jobs for the rest of his life. Having worked practically from birth he never received much of a formal education, and would work in a soft drink plant, a hamburger stand and a popsicle factory. He died in 1993 from cardiac arrest. He was 64 years old. The Spanky Club cards that he attempted to sell to my schoolmates and I had cost fifty cents. I wish that I had bought one.

Tales of Unspeakable Woe: Bingo!

Bingo! Not only was it my birthday but I had just won the game of Bingo *and* the accompanying prize, and right here at my own birthday party! I was really on a roll. If life was this terrific at seven years old, I could only imagine how much more fantastic it was going to be in, say, fifty years. Ahem.

But wait, what's going on here? Across the noisy, crowded living room my cousin Elaine was also raising her hand and yelling "Bingo!" Now what manner of subterfuge was this? Even at such a young age I knew, *everyone* knew, that when you played any game, including Bingo, you could have only one winner. And clearly the fates had already decided that winner should be *me.*

Mom and several other adults quickly checked the two Bingo cards. As hard as it was to believe, both of them were indeed winners. But the *truly* amazing part was that the two Bingo cards were absolutely identical. That two of the same card would be included in a Bingo kit and so haphazardly sold to the public was to my mind a criminal aberration so enormous in scope that I thought my young head was going to explode in outrage.

The fault, clearly, lay with some incompetent underling over at the Bingo factory. Hadn't those Bingo people ever heard of checking their work? And exactly which knucklehead over there was in charge of quality control? I wanted a name and I wanted it *now!*

Ah, but what to do? I don't remember what the prize was for winning the Bingo game, and it's entirely possible that I never knew, even then. What I *did* know was that I had won the game, fairly and squarely, and so the prize should be mine. And yet in a calmer moment I would admit that Elaine, too, had won fairly and, as much as it hurts to say it, even today, was just as entitled to the prize as was I. My, this was a puzzler, and it would take someone with the wisdom of Solomon to guide us out of this sticky conundrum. Was Mom up to the task?

Apparently not, because she shortly announced that since it was my birthday, and since I had already received a lot of presents, that it was only fair that Elaine receive the Bingo prize.

What the fuck?

No, of course I didn't utter those foul words, or even think them, but believe me the seven-year-old equivalent of the phrase, whatever that might have been, was not far from my quivering lips. I mean, what did the fact that it was my birthday, or that I had received presents, have to do with winning the Bingo game and claiming my prize? What kind of logic was that? I'm sorry Mr. Tyson, but even though you knocked your opponent into a coma we're going to declare *him* the winner...because it's your birthday. At least Solomon would have had sense enough to take his mighty sword and cut that Bingo prize right in half. Whatever it was.

Listen, I'm going to have to cut this short. I'm getting all worked up again, even though I'm fairly certain that the statute of limitations has run out on this half-century-old miscarriage of justice. I'm going to take a few deep breaths, calm down, maybe have a cup of tea. And then I'm going to send an e-mail to my cousin Elaine. I don't care how much time has gone by, that chick still owes me a prize, or at least half of one. Along with about fifty years of interest.

She Let Him Do This Often (Part I)

Dad was at work, my brothers were outside playing somewhere and Mom was upstairs taking a nap. I hoped. At least I didn't hear any tell-tale creaking of floorboards or stairs that telegraphed that she was headed down to the basement, where I, sweaty-palmed and shaking, was currently and carefully removing a musty hardcover book from the bookshelf.

The year was 1965, I was twelve and the book was *Peyton Place*. I often snuck down to the quiet of the basement to read it. Not read it cover-to-cover, mind you, but just certain parts--the "good" parts--over and over again. More on those good parts in just a bit.

Peyton Place had actually been published about a decade earlier, in 1956. I remember there was a photo of the author on the book jacket, and from that I knew she was some old lady whose last name I couldn't pronounce. Her name was Grace Metalious, and I later learned that she wrote *Peyton Place* at the age of thirty and would publish it at thirty-two. She would drink herself to death before she reached the age of forty.

At the time most first novels sold about 2,000 copies in hardcover. Peyton Place sold 60,000 within the first ten days of its release. It remained on the New York Times Best Seller list for 59 weeks. The book dealt with the sexuality of its three main characters, all women. It was pretty hot stuff for the folks back then, hopelessly stuck as they were right in the middle of the repressive Eisenhower Era.

Meanwhile back in the basement, my fingers searched feverishly for a single passage, my favorite go-to paragraph in the book. And trust that my use of the word "feverishly" is not simple hyperbole. I actually *did* feel a literal warmth, as awakening hormones surged throughout my young body as if bursting through a destroyed dam. As an adult there are still times when I once again experience this feeling, but sadly it's only when I actually *do* have a fever.

I thought about *Peyton Place* the other day, and I tried to remember what I could about some of the parts I used to read during my brief but passionate rendezvous with the classic book. This, of course, was no easy task, as my sweaty debauches in that over-heated cellar occurred nearly half a century ago.

Still, I decided to get my hands on a copy of Peyton Place and see if I could find my favorite passages, and specifically my favorite sentence, which I still remember and in fact have always remembered over the past nearly fifty years. When I was twelve I thought it was the most incredibly sexy sentence I had ever read, and to this day I'm not sure I've ever read anything else that changed my mind.

Ah, but I wonder if I remember the context of the sentence and, more importantly, do I remember that libidinous sentence accurately? And so I vow to find out. Oh, by the way, the sentence was:

She let him do this often.

She Let Him Do This Often (Part II)

It is a marvel, is it not, that you can visit Amazon.com and purchase just about any book you might desire using no more effort than a single click of a mouse? And so when I decided that I needed to track down a copy of *Peyton Place* you know where I headed. The good news was I could buy a copy of the book for as little as ninety-eight cents. The bad news was it would cost $3.99 to ship it. This would mean I could get myself a serviceable copy of *Peyton Place* for about five bucks, not an outrageous price by any means. But by now you know me well enough to accept that there was no way I was paying four dollars in order to have a ninety-eight cent book delivered to my house. Why, that's like buying a scoop of ice cream for a buck and paying four dollars more for the cone!

Sort of.

And so to the local library, where I was told that they did not have a copy of *Peyton Place*. This was no surprise, since I live in a small coastal town of about 12,000 and our library isn't exactly the New York Public-type. In fact, I suppose we should feel lucky to have any sort of library at all. Ah, but we do live in the computer age and our library is part of a county-wide system. The librarian (The prototype of which hasn't changed in fifty years, by the way.) said I could order the book and it would arrive in a few days. The catch was there would be a fee. (I knew it!) The fee was seventy-five cents. (Sweet!)

And so now if you would kindly excuse me for a bit I'm going to take my borrowed copy of Peyton Place and go in search of that sexiest of sentences. And please be patient; the book is 372 pages thick and this may take a while.

I'm back. Yes, already. Man, I wish I had brought my stopwatch and timed myself. I can't imagine it took me more than two minutes to find the sentence I was looking for, and that's with the handicap of using a different edition than the one I befouled as a horny little child. This newer softcover version was published in 1999, to honor what would have been Grace Metalious's seventy-fifth birthday, had she remained sober.

Now as I recall there was some hot action going down when that classic sentence came along. I remembered, or thought I did, that a naked woman was sitting in the driver's seat of a car while a man leaned his head in through the window and bit down, hard, on her nipple. From my memory she seemed to enjoy this quite a bit and it was this salacious act that was referred to in the sentence: *She let him do this often.*

Now remember, I had read this almost fifty years ago, so not everything was accurate. First off, let me introduce you to the happy couple, Rodney and Betty. And, while it's true that their steamy action began in a car, the part that helped get me through puberty actually happened on a beach.

"Quick!" she said. "Down on the beach. Not here."
That's our gal Betty speaking.

Perhaps the biggest surprise for me was that the magic sentence was not a sentence at all, but merely part of one; what you grammar-nazis might call an "independent clause." But when it comes to the context, my memory was dead-on. Rodney was indeed biting on one of Betty's nipples. (Which were, by the way, "always rigid and exciting." Is that even possible?) The complete sentence reads:

She let him do this often, but it never failed to arouse him to near frenzy. As I mentioned earlier, my youthful liaison with *Peyton Place* lasted only for a short period of time. One day, seemingly out of the blue, Mom casually mentioned that perhaps she should remove the scandalous book from the shelf. Whether she was worried about what visitors might think if they saw it or if by some mysterious mom-instinct she knew of my fervid and clandestine readings I don't know and never will. We never spoke of it and I didn't even find the nerve to write of it until after she died.

And then one day the book was gone from the shelf. I never again held a copy of *Peyton Place* until yesterday, when I picked it up at the library. Still, it speaks to the glory of books that after Mom, Grace Metalious and even I are long dead, the story of that twisted little New England town will go on. And for generations to come Rodney will continue to gnaw on Betty's ever-rigid nipple, and she'll always let him do this. Often.

My Friend Edelbert

I was eight years old and I was confused, which was not an uncommon circumstance for me at that age, or even at this age for that matter. But why was she calling him that?

"Edelbert!"

She did it again. The shout was coming from a window on the third floor of the old brick building that towered a short distance from my grandparents backyard. My brother and I had been dropped off at my grandparents for our usual three or four day summer visit, a visit I once believed my parents had intended as a vacation *for* us but grew to discover that it actually was a vacation *from* us.

During one of our stays we had met a neighborhood kid, became friends and generally hung around with him during our visits. He was a likable sort and his name was Eddie. The clearest memory I have of Eddie is the time he opened his wallet to show us the card he had just received in the mail. He said it was an official Archie Press Pass, and I couldn't disagree, because right there on the card it said PRESS, and next to the word was a picture of the red-headed cartoon character himself. You can't get more proof than that.

Eddie explained this was no ordinary card, but it came with privileges that I myself would probably never have, or even begin to comprehend. For example, all my friend Eddie had to do was flash his shiny new press pass and he could walk into any police station in the country. Wow! I can admit now to being supremely impressed with the card, and perhaps even just a bit jealous. It wasn't until many years later that I realized that *anybody* can walk into any police station in the country, and that walking *out* of a police station, at least in my experience, is often the more difficult part.

But what I could never understand was why, when his mother wanted him to come home, she'd lean out the window and bellow in a voice that could be heard all over the neighborhood, and probably throughout a good part of the tri-state area,

"Edelbert!'

Once I even asked my friend why his mother called him by this strange sounding name, when everybody else with half a brain knew that his name was Eddie. I don't remember his reply, because I think there really wasn't much of one, just a mumble or two, and the subject was dropped. One thing I'm *sure* he didn't say was, "Because Edelbert is my real name."

And it took an embarrassing number of years for me to figure out what was going on. I actually spent a period of time thinking that Eddie's mother must be some kind of major league moron, seeing as she didn't even seem to know her own son's name. She wasn't dumb, of course, but rather a German immigrant with roots still buried deep in the soil of the old country. Eddie, however, was pure American, and as such a steady supply of Archie comics and never again having to hear the dreaded foreign-sounding name was all he needed to be happy.

Today I did some research and discovered that Edelbert is actually a grand old Germanic name that means "nobly bright." And from what I remember of my old pal Eddie I think that fits him just fine. So wherever you are, Edelbert my friend, thanks for the memories and I'll see you at the police station.

My Favorite Christmas Present

And that's all I got--the title. In *A Christmas Story* the voice-over at the end claims that the BB gun that Ralphie finally gets is "The best present I received, the best present I would *ever* receive." It's a wonderful line and it would have been the final one in the movie had I been the editor. The sad truth is that even though we all strain our brains year after year hunting down that perfect gift to give, very few of the gifts we receive remain in our memory. Well, at least that's been my experience. Oh, I can still recall some of the presents I've gotten from the generous people who have passed through my life, but picking out a favorite? Nothing comes to mind.

Sure, I was happy enough to get that guitar when I was a kid. But it was 1964, and I certainly would have preferred an electric one as opposed to this thing they called a Spanish guitar. Why the hell did I need a Spanish guitar? The Beatles were *English*. And yes, it was nice to finally receive those Beatle boots a year later (after nearly two years of begging and whining) but it was a little late if you ask me. Hell, by the end of 1965 I doubted that the Beatles themselves were still wearing the damn things.

I certainly enjoyed the racer-style bicycle I received one year. True, it seemed like everybody else was riding those cool stingray bikes, with the banana seat and ape-hanger handlebars, but what the heck, this one was more practical, right? More traditional. I got a lot of miles out of that slick black bike, right up until the day I turned to wave to some friends and rode it smack into a cement-block wall. The bicycle's front tire and frame were bent almost beyond recognition, while I was rushed to the hospital with a concussion. Some will tell you that neither of us was ever quite right again.

Perhaps the most memorable present I ever received might sound a little goofy at first. It was a lobster tail, a gift from my girlfriend of long ago. She took a risk, I think, in giving such a present, but I understood the gift and appreciated it. And then I ate it. We were living together at the time and both working crap jobs. I liked lobster, but the odds of me even being in the same room with one over the next decade or so seemed pretty slim. And it wasn't something I'd run out to the grocery store to pick up for supper. It was a luxury gift, something you would love but wouldn't or couldn't purchase for yourself. To this day I think it was a thoughtful and clever gift. I ate most of it for dinner and finished the rest the next day. Did I share it? Oh, maybe I gave my girlfriend a taste of it, but who remembers?

This will be my 23rd Christmas with Spike. And yes, I remember the very first gifts we exchanged. But not for good reasons. During out first year together we had visited Yosemite and climbed to the top of Half Dome. I had done this twice before, but it was the first (and apparently last) time for Spike. So for Christmas I got her a framed poster of an Ansel Adams photo of Half Dome. Nice, huh? And pretty damn romantic too, I might add.

And, incidentally, at fifty bucks it was not particularly cheap. Of course to my eyes it ended up looking like just another big piece of paper when Spike handed me that 5-disc CD player. This was cutting edge technology at the time, folks. Up until that day all my music was either on vinyl or in my head. I don't know how much the gift cost, but there's no doubt it beat my romantic poster by a factor of at least three or four. Ah well, it's the thought that counts, right? Uh-huh.

Okay, I think this is the best gift I've ever *given*. It was over twenty years ago and Howard Stern had just begun broadcasting in the San Francisco area. My brother, who had been listening to Stern long before I even knew who the guy was, had moved to Florida. Florida had beautiful weather. Florida had warm, sandy beaches. But one thing Florida didn't have was Howard Stern. And so I went to the mall and forced myself to walk through the doors of the dreaded Radio Shack. There I purchased a pack of ten blank 90-minute audio cassettes and a shiny plastic carrying case. And each day I would record an hour and a half of Stern and place the completed tape in the case.

I finished the tenth one a week or so before Christmas, threw some gift wrap around the case and mailed it off to my brother. He loved it. So much in fact that I suggested that once he had listened to all the tapes he should mail them back to me and I'd fill them again. He did and I did. And then when he had finished *those* he surprised me by again returning the tapes to me, along with a simple note that read, "More, please." It was at about this point that I began to question the wisdom of my gift. Clearly I had inadvertently created a monster. Ah, but that's okay. I don't remember how many times I ended up mailing that case of tapes to Florida, but I've always been particularly proud of giving that gift. After all, what would Christmas be without crazed wack-packers, naked lesbians and fart jokes?

I Don't Want to Go to Typing Today

It was our first class of the day, right after Home Room, and both my friend Arthur and I dreaded it. Every single day. It was our high school Typing class, and within its endless forty-two minute span we were subjected to what we perceived to be the most degrading exercises that had ever been forced upon us in our short lives. Typing? We were intellectuals, for fuck's sake, not secretaries! We hated it so much that we even wrote a song we sang each day before class. It's only line was, "I don't want to go to Typing today, oh no." I'll sing it for you sometime.

You may not know by name the song "Under the Double Eagle," an Austrian Sousa-esque march from the 19th century, but you'd know it if you heard. Well, we had to listen to that crap every day, and type along to its blaring rhythm. And believe me, the last thing young hippie-types like us wanted to hear every day was some overblown and pompous military fight song. Now, if we could have typed along with, say, the *Who's Next* album, well perhaps typing class would have been more tolerable. And perhaps not.

The teacher of this class was, of course, an idiot. Oh, looking back I suppose he wasn't really, but we were seventeen years old and, as such, knew everything. Besides, the teacher (and don't think for a minute that I don't remember his name) also taught driver education, so perhaps our youthful impressions of him were more accurate than my middle-aged guilt will allow me to admit today. I can still recall him dictating to the class as we practiced our "home row" keys (once that horrible music had mercifully ended) "J-J-J-Space and K-K-K-Space." And who can forget that historic Monday when this teacher stood in front of the class confessing he'd had a horrible weekend because he'd spent it "digging a grave for a dog." Arthur and I were just about bursting in joyous disbelief.

And yet we somehow made it through the year attending our typing class, just as we had with all of our other high school classes. Classes which included such lofty subjects as American History, Chemistry, Geometry, Calculus, Biology, Drama and so many more. And as I sit here now, hunched over my trusty, dusty keyboard, I never could have imagined that the torturous class that Arthur and I suffered through every day while making fun of the poor dope up front who was simply trying to earn a living would, with the unforeseen rise of the personal computer, turn out to be the most valuable class I ever took.

Snow

I like snow. I've written before about the many disappointing mornings I experienced as a kid when I woke up and looked out on a wet, gray street after a major snowfall had been predicted the night before. And about the unbridled joy of that snowstorm that turned the world white on one magical Christmas Eve so long ago.

What is it I like about snow? Well, it's certainly not shoveling it. I remember as a kid hearing stories about men of a certain age collapsing with heart attacks while shoveling the white stuff. And now I *am* that certain age. And I certainly don't enjoy the cold that accompanies the snow. No, I think what I like most about snow is looking at it; especially watching it come down. Especially from inside the house.

And yet it's been over thirty years since I've lived in a place where it snows. Or at least where it snows on a regular basis. Last week there were reports of the snow level falling to 1500 feet here in the Bay Area. There was even footage on TV of big white fluffy flakes coming down in the Santa Cruz Mountains and in Berkeley. I was hoping that it might even snow here in Half Moon Bay, but since the elevation is a non-lofty 70 feet above sea level it seemed unlikely.

Still, I felt like I wanted to see some snow come down, so I made the drive up the hill. To get from the coast, where I live, to the bay about twenty minutes away you have to drive over the mountain ridge that runs like a spine down the peninsula, a ridge that in spots is over the 1500-foot level. One night last week I saw people driving down from these mountains with their cars dusted with snow. So the next day when more snow was predicted I got in my car and headed for the short drive up the hill.

About half an hour later I was seeing little patches of white by the side of the road, leftovers from the previous day's snow. Each patch contained just about enough snow for constructing one, possibly two good-sized snowballs. A few minutes later I rounded a turn and it was snowing! It wasn't exactly a blizzard, the flakes were fat and soggy and surely melted the second they hit the ground if not before, but it was snowing! I pulled over to the side of the road, got out of the car, and walked for a while amidst the pine trees while bits of falling snow danced around me. Occasionally a car drove by and I suspect that when the people inside exclaimed, "Look, there's another flake!" they weren't talking about the snow.

Spike and I were watching the news last week when they predicted a major snowstorm for New York City. And as I do at so many things, I scoffed. "You just watch," I said in my all-knowing yet seldom accurate way. "Tomorrow they'll be talking about how the storm wasn't nearly as big as expected and how New York had dodged a bullet." I've had years of experience with that group—I know how they work.

When I was a kid in the New York area any snowfall of more than a foot was a major storm. So when they announced that New York City had received over *two* feet of snow, well, I knew that the "I told you so!" that I had prepared would remain firmly wedged in my throat, with no chance of ever seeing the light of day. And if I still harbored any thoughts that I had not been completely and colossally wrong in my prediction, the man on the TV set me straight by announcing that it was the biggest snowfall in New York City since *before the Civil War*. Ahem.

The previous record snowfall for New York City had also been over two feet, and had occurred in 1947. I was talking to my mom on the phone when the subject of New York's big snow came up. When I mentioned the 1947 storm she said she knew about it. In fact she remembered it.

She and my dad, who wasn't yet my dad at the time, were actually just dating. The historic marriage that ended up bestowing me upon the world was still three years off. They had plans to go into the city to see a show or a movie. My mom wasn't quite sure which they did on that day. It was a different time then—those two folks who would become my parents frequently took the train into the city to see live shows, plays and movies. Sometimes they would see two in one day. People could afford that back then, as a live show and dinner for two would cost about eight cents. OK, I forget the actual price, but it *was* inexpensive.

So, whatever form of entertainment my future parents went to that day, when they emerged from the theater it was snowing. Hard. Just as it had been predicted, although predicted by what means I can't imagine. Town crier? My mom's mom, my wonderful Italian grandma now long gone, had warned her not to go out because a big storm was coming. My mom, nineteen years old and apparently carrying the "stubborn asshole" gene that she would later pass on to her firstborn, had ignored the warning and would now pay the price.

It took hours for the adventurous young couple to get home. Even when they were finally able to catch a train that brought them to somewhere near their home (They lived in the same town, not the same house, you sickos. People didn't do that in 1947. Not *my* parents, anyway.) they still faced a three or four mile walk once they left the warmth and safety of the train. And it was my grandma who greeted my mom at the door when she, cold and exhausted, finally made it home. "I told you so!" said Grandma, and believe me, that was one "I told you so!" that I bet didn't stick in the throat.

And how does my mom look at this near-disaster from the vantage point of sixty years later; a night when a young couple with their whole lives ahead of them huddled arm in arm and struggled home for miles through the falling snow? "It's a nice memory," she says.

I like snow.

Look Back in Hunger

I read this formula a while back theorizing that the age of a man is roughly equivalent to the percentage of men who are bald at that particular age. Yeah, I know, huh? Let me clear it up for you. This formula claims that about thirty percent of thirty-year-old men are bald, forty percent of forty-year-old men, half of fifty-year-old men and so on. It sounds like nonsense to me, but who knows? After all, it's just a rough rule of thumb. I mean, ten percent of ten-year-old boys are not bald, nor are all hundred-year-old men. You know what? Forget I even brought it up. What I planned on writing about tonight is the school lunches we used to get in grade school. How the hell am I going to segue from bald men to school lunches? Watch and learn, children.

I've recently come up with my own formula that probably has as much basis in fact as the above bald man theory. That is, none whatsoever. *My* theory claims that the age of a person (and yes, you ladies can play along in this one) directly corresponds to the percentage of time one spends thinking about the past. You still with me? In other words, a twenty-year-old will only spend about twenty per cent of his time thinking about the past, while a seventy-year-old will spend seventy percent of the time thinking about the past. And the hundred-year-old? Sadly, he thinks about nothing but.

What led to the creation of this insightful theory was noticing that I had been repeatedly thinking about the past, or more specifically, one particular aspect of the past. And no it's not about regrets or lost loves or any of that morbid auld lang syne crap. For some reason I've been thinking about the school lunches I used to eat when I was in grade school. (Wham! Did you see that? From bald men to school lunches in three short paragraphs! Man, am I something or what?)

The main thing I remember about the school lunches we had in grade school is that they were so damn good! To this day I can distinctly remember the look and the taste of at least five or six different meals that the good cafeteria ladies would serve. No lie: Just now my memory conjured up a ghostly whiff of a grilled cheese sandwich that was served forty years ago. Spooky, huh?

Once a month the school would print a menu, and I can still remember the tantalizing way that the descriptions were worded. "Barbeque Beef on Buttered Bun." "Spaghetti with meat sauce, cheese and Italian bread." "Chow mein with noodles, rice." Jesus Christ, I just remembered what the *bread* that came with the spaghetti looked and tasted like! And now I remember the incredible French dressing on the salad. Boy things really stay with you, don't they? No wonder I can't get those fucking catechism questions out of my head.

There were two kinds of kids back then: those who *brought* their lunch and those who *bought* their lunch. In the vernacular you were known as either a Hot Lunch or a

Cold Lunch, wording which smacks less of class distinction than the Haves and Have-Nots, don't you think? For the longest time we, my brothers and I, were Cold Lunches. We'd bring our sandwiches and cookies and a piece of fruit to school in a brown bag every day. I can still remember sitting in class around eleven o'clock, listening to some teacher drone on endlessly about some arcane subject that I've long since forgotten, as the fumes from my baloney and catsup sandwich wafted from the brown bag and toward my accepting nostrils, like beckoning finger-shaped smoke tendrils from some classic old cartoon.

No, for a long time we were not to be counted among the Hot Lunch people. Who could afford it? The Hot Lunch back then, including milk and dessert, cost a whopping thirty cents! And I swear to you this is not being written by some eighty-year-old man. (Who has but twenty percent of his hair.) Sure, scoff now, but figure three kids, a buck a day, twenty-plus bucks a month. It adds up. And that's 1960's dollars, chump. Baloney was *definitely* the fiscally responsible way to go.

Then around fifth grade everything changed. Either my mom finally grew weary of making three lunches a day, *every* day, or my dad finally got off his lazy butt and *got* that third job in order to feed his three growing Baby Hueys. But for whatever the reason, we suddenly became Hot Lunch People. And these then are the lunches, despite my having since eaten countless wonderful meals in restaurants all over the world, that have stayed in my head for over forty years.

I still remember the spaghetti. It was fatter than average (Who wasn't?) and completely filled the plastic blue-green plate on which it was served. A generous amount of parmesan cheese always dusted the top, and of course you've already met the bread. The cheeseburgers tasted charbroiled, because they probably were. I don't know if the chow mein bore any relationship to actual Asian cuisine, but boy it was good. The barbequed beef was delicious, and always had one little piece of cooked celery in it, which, incredibly, was also delicious!

When they finally do invent that time machine for home use, one of the first things I'm going to do (after subjecting the young Barbara Bush to a mandatory sterilization, of course) is to go back to my grade school, plunk down thirty cents and have lunch. I'm truly curious to learn if the culinary treats I remember would be quite as appealing to the middle-aged palate as apparently they were to a child's.

Sadly, I've heard that my old grade school no longer exists; or rather it has been greatly expanded into some monstrous office complex built to serve the whims of the school district. That's unfortunate, because I think the board really missed an opportunity here. I believe they would have been better served to convert that old school into a restaurant. I, for one, certainly would have eaten there. Especially on barbeque beef day.

The Night My Brother Fell In Love

For this one we'll have to set the way-back machine to well over two decades ago. Let's call it 1983. My brother and I had taken a trip together to Hawaii and as we pick up the action it's a balmy tropical night that finds us in the hotel suite that we were renting on the island of Kauai.

My brother was in the living room and I was lying down in the bedroom staring at the ceiling. Both of us were whacked out of our minds on some of the local product. I had shared a joint earlier in the day with a local grower I had met, and had been nice enough to pocket the roach in order to share it later on with my brother. Yes, we were both in a near-catatonic state from simply having shared a single roach. People will tell you that grass wasn't that powerful back then, but this stuff remains the strongest I've ever smoked and hopefully the strongest I ever will.

My body may have been deadly still on that hotel bed but my mind was soaring among the stars, fluttering from planet to planet like a moth at a light bulb convention. I heard no sound coming from the living room except for a thin layer of background music from the television. Suddenly I heard my brother's voice and my mind immediately was whipped back into my body like a snapped bungee cord. With no small amount of effort I rose from the bed, steadied myself and plodded into the living room.

"What did you say?" I muttered. Looking back, it's more probable that I said, "Did you say something?" After all, although I knew I had heard a voice, in my current condition I couldn't be sure from where it had originated. All I knew for sure was that *somebody* had spoken to me.

"This chick," said my brother, his drooping eyelids valiantly attempting to protect a pair of bloodshot eyes. "She's kind of weird, but there's something really attractive about her."

I directed my gaze at the flickering TV screen and attempted to focus. MTV. My brother had been watching music videos while I had been space traveling. Then I focused a little more and zeroed in the object of my brother's newfound lust. Oh, good God.

"So you think she's pretty hot?" I asked, or something that was roughly the 1983 equivalent. I'm not sure that we described people as "hot" back then unless they had a fever.

"Yeah, I know she's strange looking but I think she's real sexy."

"Uh yes, you'd make a lovely couple, "I sighed and then lowered the sound on the TV and turned to face my brother.

I was, after all, the older one, and as such felt it my responsibility to help guide him through some of life's confusing moments. Still, I must confess to being a little surprised, as my brother was always the one who was much more aware of the newer, more current music. I on the other hand was, and continue to be, hopelessly and blissfully stuck in the music of the sixties. And it was for this reason that I simply could not believe that my brother had never before seen, or even heard of, Boy George.

After The Sun Sets

In front of me I've placed a book called *After The Sun Sets*. I know it sounds like erotica, but it is not. It's actually a book that I've owned for decades, since childhood in fact, and yet knew exactly where on the bookshelf to find it tonight.

Many old books smell wonderful; a dusty blend of intellect and time. This one, however, does not. In fact it kind of stinks and I'm looking forward to finishing this article so I can return it to the shelf, perhaps for another decade or two.

The book is brown and fairly beat up. And, much like a Democratic congressman, the spine is missing. Under the title on the front cover, is a two-color depiction of a knight charging on a horse. There is a line below the illustration that tells me that *After The Sun Sets* is one of The Wonder-Story Books, whatever the hell they are. I mean, were.

Inside the three hundred page book is a collection of stories, most of which have been known to us in one form or another since we were children. Hansel and Gretel, Cinderella, and Snow White all make appearances. There are also some lesser-known characters; for example, who the hell is Aiken-Drum the Brownie? Who cares, he's probably dead by now.

After The Sun Sets is not just some ordinary book that I've carried with me for most of my life. No, it is so much more. In fact it is a book that I've felt guilty about owning ever since it was given to me nearly half a century ago.

This happened in either first or second grade. Let's say first. Our teacher, Mrs. Clerk, had to leave for some unexplained reason, and so our class was shuffled across the hall to be combined for a few hours with the other first grade class. Mrs. Clerk had warned us to behave while she was gone and reminded us that we were, in fact, guests in this new classroom. And so she left, but not before delivering a final promise: When she returned she would have a present for each of us; at least for those of us who hadn't needed to be "spoken to" by our temporary teacher.

A short time later I was sitting in a chair in the over-crowded classroom, listening attentively to this unknown teacher, relaxed with my hands clasped behind my head. I must have looked a little *too* relaxed for this rigid 1950's-style educator, because suddenly the impossible happened.

"You! Yes, you! Put your arms down!"

I was stunned. I lowered my arms as told, but my mind was racing. Why was this teacher talking to me in this sharp manner? I was, after all, a star pupil. Didn't she know that? And, worst of all, had I just been "spoken to"?

My brain was still in a confused anguish when Mrs. Clerk returned and herded us back into our home classroom. And then she asked the question:

"Was anybody spoken to while I was gone?"

One kid whose name is lost in the foggy recesses raised his hand, and this was no surprise to anybody including

Mrs. Clerk. I may not remember this child's name, but I do recall that he was a complete fuck-up.

"Anybody else?" Mrs. Clerk asked.

Of course I couldn't raise my hand, and it was not that I so desperately wanted whatever gift Mrs. Clerk was planning on handing out. It was that I didn't belong in that "bad student" category. Why, had I confessed, I frantically justified, it might give an old lady like Mrs. Clerk (she was probably about 35) a heart attack. I was, after all, one of her prize pupils.

And besides, exactly what did it mean to be "spoken to" anyway? She should have more clearly defined her parameters. My only surprise was the silence of my classmates. I truly expected one of them to snitch at any minute, or at least bring up the incident for a class discussion. But nobody did. And my arm remained at my side.

This incident took place around 1960. *After The Sun Sets* was published in 1938, and so each of us "good" students was rewarded with their very own copy of a 22-year old book, a book that had obviously been discontinued by the New York City Board of Education.

That then is the end of the story and so finally I can take this now nearly 70-year old book and return it, along with its foul odor, to the dark obscurity of my bookshelf. And no, the boy who *had* confessed did not receive a copy.

I Remember Gladys M. Gilgar

But just barely. Gladys M. Gilgar was an old lady who owned a greeting card and stationery store in my hometown when I was growing up, which as we all know was quite some time ago. I am reminded of her each time I am forced to shell out three or four dollars for a greeting card at Hallmark.

On these occasions I never miss an opportunity to regale the bored, minimum wage-earning clerk with stories about how when I was a child you had a choice of two prices for greeting cards: ten cents or fifteen cents. Oh, how the young people enjoy hearing rambling, seemingly pointless yarns about the olden days from a leering, AARP-eligible reprobate such as myself!

Now when I tell these tales I don't mention Gladys M. Gilgar, but that's where I used to buy the cards. We didn't have Hallmark stores back then. Hell, we didn't even have a mall. We had shops, dammit, and Gladys M. Gilgar's was about a mile from my home, about twenty minutes by bicycle.

I mentioned that Gladys M. Gilgar was an old lady, but as we all eventually discover some of the people we remember from our youth as being positively ancient turn out to have been in their thirties or forties when we look back. That said, I'm still reasonably certain that Gladys M. Gilgar was old. Real old.

I remember that one of the worst mistakes you could make after you entered Gladys M. Gilgar's shop was to ask her for something. One thing the regulars knew is that you didn't ask Gladys M. Gilgar anything. Not if you wanted to be back out on the street within the next hour or so.

If you asked Gladys M. Gilgar where the birthday cards were, for example, she wouldn't just tell you. Gladys M. Gilgar, sweet old lady that she was, would insist on coming over to show you. And believe me, even in that tiny shop, this trek took a long time. And nothing you could say could dissuade her. No amount of "That's OK, I'll find it" or "Oh, here it is!" could turn back Gladys M. Gilgar once she had begun her shuffling journey.

And yes, what I mentioned earlier was quite true. You basically had a choice of either being a cheapskate and buying a ten-cent card, or going whole hog and splurging for the fifteen-cent number. As I remember, one of the main factors was how you might be feeling towards the planned recipient of the card on that given day. Did you have a fight with your brother two days before his birthday? Did your parents force you to get a particularly short haircut a week before their anniversary? If so, then there was clearly a ten-cent card in their immediate future.

But your emotional state on the day you went card shopping at Gladys M. Gilgar's was not the only factor determining which price card you would choose. It might not seem like a big deal now, but remember back then there was a lot a kid could do with a nickel. In fact you could buy an entire Hershey's chocolate bar for a nickel. And not one of those miniscule "fun size" things you can still sometimes get for a quarter today. I'm talking about a full-size candy bar.

So now the choices get more intriguing, eh? You could either walk into Gladys M. Gilgar's and buy your poor, hard-working mother a beautifully frilly birthday card for fifteen cents, or for the same fifteen cents you could get a perfectly acceptable birthday for your mother *and* a full-sized Hershey's candy bar for yourself.

Did I ever mention that I was kind of a pudgy kid?

That Championship Season

I suppose it was all the excitement over the current baseball play-offs that reawakened the memories. Or maybe it was just another example of the random, haphazard manner in which my brain, and yours too, operates. Whatever the reasons I today recalled a day that happened a long time ago during my first of two stints as a member of a Little League team.

The details are sketchy at best, and probably contain inaccuracies besides. So what? I'm not a journalist and there's nobody around to correct me anyway. As I said, this happened a very long time ago.

I know I was in second grade at the time so that would put my age at what, seven? I also know that this was the first time I had played for any organized team or had worn a team uniform. (Correction: I had two years earlier owned a hot, itchy New York Yankees uniform. I had asked my Mom if she could sew a number 7 onto the uniform, and when she didn't respond quickly enough a friend of hers said she would do it. Which she never did. In fact neither one of those broads ever sewed that number 7 on my little Yankee uniform. As you can tell I'm still a little miffed about that, but next year, seeing how it will be the 50th anniversary of that brutal soul-scarring refusal, I may be willing to forgive the crime and get on with my life. And then again I may not.)

Before the Little League season began there was a parade in which all the teams would march. I remember as we began to march one young punk on the team directly in front of us turned and asked the name of our team.

"The Braves," responded one of my teammates.

"Ha!" laughed the evil little bastard. "They should call you the *Chickens.*"

And somehow, although we had yet to play a single inning or even hold a practice, I knew he was right. I instinctively knew that the fates had landed me on what would prove to be the crappiest team in the league. I also seemed to know that this was something I had better get used to in life. And, for the most part, I have.

But I'm not here to wallow in the miserable season that the Chick—I mean the *Braves* struggled through that year. I don't really remember very much about it, except for one particularly painful game when we lost to a team sponsored by a local gas station called Marty's Esso. The final score was 18-2. Ouch.

Ah, but this is not a story of gloom and defeat, but rather a tale of personal triumph. More specifically, it's about *my* personal triumph. It's about the best day I had as a member of the Braves. It was a day that for the first (and only) time as the sorriest member of that sorry team that I felt an emotion that resembled something close to "pride." It was the day I got a hit.

Again I ask you to bear with me because the details are vague at best, and becoming more vague each year. I don't know how many games we played that season.

Eight? Ten? I don't recall if we won any, although I'm pretty sure that we didn't. I don't even remember what position I played though I suspect I had been banished to right field, where I would do the least amount of damage. And I don't remember how many at bats I had over the course of the season.

What I *do* remember is that before this magical day late in the season I had not gotten any hits. Nope, not a single one. And not only had I failed to reach base safely even once, I also was never throw out or had a fly ball of mine caught. Yes, up until this day I had *never even once made contact with the ball.* Which means, of course, that I had struck out every single time I was at bat! I'm not even sure whether I ever even hit a foul ball or tipped one, but I'm fairly sure that I did not. Pretty pathetic, huh?

Ah but this day would be different. As I stepped up to the plate and as the first pitch approached me I saw that it was unique. Never before had I been able to see a pitch so clearly, to track it so accurately. There could have been numerous reasons why this was so, but even today I know the truth of the situation. No, my skill or eye-hand coordination hadn't suddenly improved. My practice batting sessions weren't about to pay off either. The reason this pitch was different was because it was coming in real s-l-o-w. Or, in other words, the kid pitching on the mound stank.

I can't say for sure, of course, but I'd bet half my 401K that I swung at the first pitch this kid threw. Who could resist with the ball floating in like a cloud and looking about the size of a watermelon? And then "crack!" I hit it!

I would ask you all to please stop here and kindly lower your expectations. Did you imagine that I had sent the ball deep into left field and over the fence for a homerun? Let's get real, shall we? I never actually did see where the ball went but I was able to deduce that it trickled back to the pitcher.

What happened next I didn't know then and I still don't. Did the pitcher muff the play and drop the ball before he could throw it to first, thus committing an error? Perhaps, but I don't want to know about it. All I know is that when the dust had settled I was standing safely at first base and just about bursting with pride. Yes, three quarters of the way through this miserable season the improbable had happened: I had gotten a hit.

And now the story gets better and even a little strange. As I stepped up for my next time at bat I was a little saddened to discover that I would be facing a different pitcher. And yet I became more hopeful when it turned out that this new pitcher was *the twin brother* of the guy off whom I had gotten my hit. I'm not kidding!

And, glory be to God, he threw *exactly* the same as his brother; that is, like an 85-year-old arthritic! And so once again the pitch floated in, again I swung and again I connected. And again the ball trickled back to the pitcher. The twin must have been a better fielder than his brother however, and despite my best efforts to race down the baseline for the second time that afternoon (and the second time that season) I was, alas, thrown out at first.

And yet being out at first hardly seemed to matter. I was giddy with the success of my day. I had hit the ball twice and almost, almost had gotten two hits. For someone who had struck out during his previous ten or fifteen times at bat this was like single-handedly winning the World Series. Perhaps even then I knew I would never forget the feeling as I stood on first base after my hit, trying to act cool as I listened to the smattering of applause I was hearing for the first (and last) time that season. And it felt wonderful. And it still does forty-six years later.

Of course by the next game things for me had returned to the familiar and humiliating status quo. I never did come close to getting another hit during that first Little League season. How could I? I never got a chance to bat against those chicken-armed twins again.

The Day Gladys M. Gilgar Yelled At Me

So now you're all familiar with Gladys M. Gilgar. If you're not, well then you've got some work to do, don't you? Go back and read the above essay about Gladys, and when you're done we'll be here waiting for you. Go on, scat!

I just rediscovered some photos of myself taken during my puberty years, and a person who looks more utterly uncomfortable in his own skin I never hope to see. The pictures make it painfully obvious that I indeed had an awkward adolescence. And since I also had an awkward childhood, and am currently dragging myself through an awkward middle age, I therefore see no imaginable way that I'll be able to avoid an awkward old age.

I remember on this particular day I had purchased a greeting card from Gladys M. Gilgar, though whether it was the ten-cent or fifteen-cent variety I can't say for sure. I was back outside and was walking towards my bicycle with a friend when I suddenly remembered that I hadn't said Thank You to Gladys M. Gilgar when I had paid for the card.

This may not seem like a big deal now but at the time, while not exactly devastating, the oversight made me feel more than a little bad. I had been raised to use those magic words "please" and "thank you" and still do to this day. Probably to excess, but I honestly believe that they continue to add a desperately needed sprinkle of civility to a world that has gone horribly, horribly wrong.

I can't imagine that my friend would have thought less of me because I didn't thank Gladys M. Gilgar, but the rude mistake was weighing heavy on my young mind. And as I have often done in the past when something has made me uncomfortable I made a joke about it.

"Well, you know what I always say, " I announced to my friend in a boastful voice that belied the meek little heart inside, " When you have to pay for something you don't have to say thank you!" Ha! Good one! Well not really, but after all I was just trying to expunge the guilt I was feeling for my callous act, not start a stand-up career. Inside I knew that this pompous outburst was not the real me and did not reflect how I truly felt inside.

I knew it, but Gladys M. Gilgar, who had left the store directly behind me, didn't. And now she let me have it. "You should *always* say thank you, young man, even if you pay for something!" she yelled in a voice that was louder and projected further than you would have expected from the bent-over, little old lady that was Gladys M. Gilgar.

I'm not sure what I did next. A lot of times, even as a child, when verbally attacked I would immediately go into defense mode. I might not do anything more than mutter a terse, "Mind your own business," under my breath but I was still filled with anger and righteous indignation. Not this time. I most likely blushed, said nothing and rode away on my bicycle as fast as I could. Why? Because this time I knew that Gladys M. Gilgar was right.

I Booed Roy Campanella

I couldn't have been more than five years old. Dad had taken me to a ballgame, although I don't recall at which ballpark. I *do* remember that it was an "exhibition game," because it was a phrase I had never heard before and was having trouble understanding the concept. The novelty of this particular game was that the Yankees were playing the Dodgers. In those days the only time a National League team would play against an American League team was in the World Series, unless, of course, they had one of these exhibition games. Whatever that meant.

Now I may have been just a kid but there was one thing I knew for sure: I was a Yankee fan. Hey, I was five years old—I didn't know any better. When I was a child I thought as a child, and all that. (I eventually grew up, started to think straight and switched to the Mets.) Now Dad, he was a Dodger fan, and although the team had left Brooklyn the year before I guess he still needed a team to root for while awaiting the creation of the Mets, which was still four years away.

I remember that it was cold that night, but I wasn't going to let that dampen my enthusiasm. I clapped and cheered as each Yankee was introduced, and I booed with an equivalent energy for every Dodger. And then they introduced Roy Campanella and I booed him. Yes, in 1958 I booed Roy Campanella.

A little background. Roy Campanella began his major league career in 1948 as the first black catcher in history. He played ten seasons with the Brooklyn Dodgers and was voted the National League's Most Valuable Player in three of those years. He played in five World Series and was selected for the All-Star team in eight of his ten seasons. In January of 1958 he was in a car crash that ended his career in baseball. In fact he never walked again and spent the remainder of his life in a wheelchair.

Well, hell, *I* didn't know that! I had never even heard of him. I was *five years old*, for crissake! And so when he was introduced I booed him as I would have any other Dodger. My actions, I imagine, painted quite a pretty picture to those fans who were lucky enough to be seated near me. These same fans were giving Campanella a standing ovation, which was another problem. How was I expected to know the guy was in a wheelchair when I couldn't even *see* him? After all, I was only about three feet tall at the time.

Finally my Dad, who must have been mortified and rightfully so, said something to me. I don't remember his words, but it might have been something along the lines of, "He's in a *wheelchair*." I do, however, remember my reply. I also remember that it was not delivered with malice, but only as an attempt to cover up both my horrible error *and* my extreme embarrassment.

"So what? He's still a Dodger."

Roy Campanella was elected to Baseball's Hall of Fame in 1969 and his #39 was retired by the Dodgers in

1972. He died in 1993, having spent nearly half his life in a wheelchair. And I, dopey little kid that I was, had booed him. I had booed Roy Campanella just three months after his crippling accident. Jesus, I hope he didn't hear me.

Made in the USA
Monee, IL
10 June 2024

59732769R00105